CHILDREN'S MINISTRY CURRICI

CHARITY SERIES
BIBLE STUDY

DocUmeant Publishing

Published by
DocUmeant Publishing
244 5th Avenue, Suite G-200
NY, NY 10001

646-233-4366

Designed and formatted by Ginger Marks, DocUmeantDesigns.com

LCCN: pending

ISBN: 9781950075874

Curriculum for
Children's Ministry Leaders

Introduction

The Charity Series is a creation of Heaven's Divine Kiss. Together, the Charity Series and Bible Study Curriculum will address the difficult topics that young people face and adults find challenging to discuss.

Charity, who is symbolic of God's love, enhances each lesson. She is a heart-shaped character who is heaven-sent to assist children in dealing with their various challenges. Charity, with the assistance of her brother, Champ, serve as God's agents of love and comfort during difficult times.

With Charity as a visual image to showcase God's kiss (affection), children will eagerly embrace every lesson.

Let me **introduce** myself

STEPHANIE A. KILGORE-WHITE is a inspirational speaker, licensed Children and Youth minister, former missionary with Campus Crusade for Christ, and a retired teacher. She graduated from Appalachian State University with a bachelor's degree in special education.

White possesses a passion for communicating the gospel to people of all ages, but her mission is to share God's love with children. It is clear that God has orchestrated her life with intention and divine purpose—to impact the hearts of young people for Him. She does this through her Heaven's Divine Kiss and Charity book series of which she is the author and illustrator.

Stephanie currently resides in McDonough, Georgia with her husband, Jerry, and is a mother of four.

Course **Program.**

SECTION

Backgound

This section introduces the ministry and mission of the beloved character Charity. It will also highlight the overall objectives and intended outcome of each lesson.

Page vi

SECTION

Lessons

Section two will explore biblical studies that will highlight the many ways in which God's love is demonstrative in the lives of biblical characters. It will also reveal how God is currently at work in extending His love to children as they are faced with life's most challenging situations.

Page 5

SECTION

Activities & Resources

Section three provides unlimited hours of fun, engaging and academic enriching activities that brings clarity to each lesson.

Page 69

Section 1

The word Charity means love in its highest form. It signifies the reciprocal love between God and mankind, which He in turns desires for each us to express to others. This love is best described in 1 Corinthians 13. It is the kind of love that outperforms any talk or speech, word, knowledge, or intention. It is demonstrated in action.

Love, in its truest sense, displays patience and kindness. It is not selfish or rude but seeks to put others and their needs above its own. It applauds the accomplishments of its opponents. It is slow to show anger and quick to extend forgiveness and grace. It is never unjust but acts justly towards people of various backgrounds, religions, or race. It is a lasting love under all kinds of circumstances and endures to the end. Charity displays unconditional love despite the effort of others.

Read: *Presenting Charity and Champ*

Charity means love!

Lesson Objective

This series will build confidence and help children discover God's love and affection, displayed as a kiss, through the many challenges they face. Students will realize that they are not alone in their struggles, but have a caring comforting friend, who will strengthen them amidst their most difficult times.

Introduction / Pre-Lesson for Leaders.

The overall purpose of Charity and Champ is to be a visual presence in the lives of children who are struggling and in need of God's comfort and care. The two are heaven-sent to address the difficulties of life and to signify God's ever-present concerns at just the right time. They minister His love and kindness amidst life's challenges. They address issues like:

1. Troubles in the home leading to abuse
2. The struggles that come from having a single mom who is overwhelmed with the cares of life
3. Struggles in school that arise from being bullied
4. Long term sicknesses that confines a child to their home
5. The frustrations of having dad absent from one's life
6. The need to belong to a family when abandoned by both parents
7. The grief that comes from losing a loved one
8. Self-esteem issues when feeling rejected
9. Discrimination due to one's skin color
10. And more . . .

Charity and Champ's mission is to point children to Jesus. It's their desire to help children realize that God is just a prayer away. The goal is to reveal how much He cares and that they are not alone in their struggles. Not only will He be present during the tough times, but He will guide, comfort, protect and provide what is needed to help them endure.

This curriculum is packed with God's word and will point students to examples in scripture of people who have encountered similar situations. The biblical examples are relatable and easy for children to understand the presence and power of God. The overall objective is that students will connect with the stories in the bible and will embrace a loving caring Father, who they will willingly place their faith and trust.

At the beginning of each lesson recite the following poem.

Charity Means Love

Charity and Champ are sent from above,

To share with you,

the message of God's amazing love.

C-H-A-R-I-T-Y means LOVE.

Also discuss with them how much God loves them.

Theme Song: Listen to "God's Love is Big" (https://youtu.be/ss-qCvdMAmc)

The key verse to be recited at the beginning of each lesson is Ephesians 3:16-20 (NLT)

*"I pray that from his glorious unlimited resources he will empower you with inner strength through His Spirit. Then Christ will make his home in your hearts as you trust in him. Your roots will grow down into God's love and keep you strong. And may you have the power to understand, as all God's people should, how <u>wide</u>, how <u>long</u>, how <u>high</u> and how <u>deep</u> his **love** is. May you experience the **love** of Christ, though it is too great to understand fully. Then you will be made complete with all the fullness of life and power that comes from God."*

"But I consider my life of no value to myself; my purpose is to finish my course in the ministry I received from the Lord Jesus, to testify to the gospel of God's grace" (Acts 20:24).

Section

Lesson 1

A Friend in Need

Topic: Friendship
Scripture: 1 Samuel 18:1–4 and 2 Chronicles 20:7

The first book of the series will allow students to be aware of God's ongoing presence in their lives. They will come away knowing that God is trustworthy and will be a forever friend whom they can always depend.

LESSON 1: A FRIEND IN NEED

How many of you have a close friend? What is it about your friend that makes him/her special to you? Why did you choose this person to be your friend?

The bible says in Proverbs 17:17 that "a friend loves you at all times". No matter what you do, or fail to do, a true friend will be loyal to you till the end of time.

In 1 Samuel, we read about a special friendship between Jonathan and David. Jonathan is the son of King Saul. His father, Saul was the first man to be selected as King in the bible. King Saul had witnessed the young teen David, defeat a giant named Goliath. While everyone else fled from the challenge to go up against Goliath, young David was bold and courageous. He was victorious at defeating this giant of a man with just three small stones and a sling shot.

King Saul was quite impressed with David's courage and boldness and invited him to his home. He gave David a job in his military army, even though; David was too young to be a soldier, the King appointed him to serve. In verse 5, it says, David marched with the King's army and was successful in everything Saul sent him to accomplish.

Jonathan, King Saul's son, had also witnessed David's victory in defeating Goliath and admired his courage as well. He instantly bonded with David when he came to work for his dad. Although Jonathan was older than David, he had a strong admiration for his boldness and courageous acts. The two became close friends and made a covenant with one another that nothing or no one would ever come between their brotherhood.

As a son of the King, Jonathan was to be the successor of the royal throne. He had already been given a robe and all the accessories that would come with his awaited position to the throne. However, because he became informed of David's anointing to later become king, and the special call that God had placed on his life, he handed over his robe and accessories to him.

How many of you would be willing to give something that belong to you to your closest friend? Would you be willing to celebrate your friend's success, even if they outshined you in the things that they do?

Jonathan did just that. His father quickly became jealous of David due to the people's praise of his accomplishments, however, Jonathan stayed true to his friendship with David, even when his dad threatened to take his friend's life. He stayed loyal to his friendship to the very end.

Friends may come and go, but a special friendship will stay true and loyal no matter what occurs in life. In Proverbs 18:24 it says, "a good friend will stick closer than a brother."

In the beginning of this book, *A Need for a Friend*, Diamond is sad and lonely. God recognizes her need and sends Charity, a special agent of His love, to befriend Diamond.

The two develop an instant bond as they spend time daily seeking to help others in need. Through their acts of kindness, Diamond experiences what it is like to have a loyal friend.

Even though her time with Charity is short lived, she treasures the experiences they shared and she learns a valuable lesson that teaches her how to focus on the needs of others around her.

Diamond discovers a newly found joy, which brings her fulfillment. As a result, she is no longer focused on being lonely, instead she becomes fully aware of God's love and His ability to meet all her needs. This includes a need for a friend, which leads her to fully embrace a desire to live her life with purpose.

Charity Acts.

Whenever you are feeling lonely, turn the focus off yourself and ask God to help you reach out to someone who is in need. Call someone who you could befriend or lend a helping hand.

Think of ways you could be a Charity to someone in need. Share God's kiss.

Charity Activities.

- Make a friendship bracelet and give it to a friend.

- Make a flower and write on the petals character traits that make a friend. (see template on page 113)

Song: "I am a Friend of God"
Sing the song in rounds: "Make New Friends, But Keep the Old, One is Silver and the Other's Gold"

Parent Resource for Child Experiencing Loneliness

7 Ways Parents Can Help Kids
Cope with Loneliness
Joe DiMaggio Children's Hospital (jdch.com)

Lesson 2
Loving the Skin I'm In

Topic: I Am Who You Say I Am
Scripture: Psalm 139:13–16

Memory verse
"... I have been remarkably and wondrously made" (Psalms 139:14).

Read: *Loving the Skin I'm In*

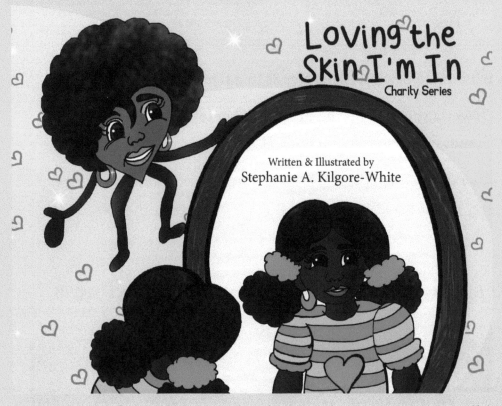

The second book of the Charity series deals with acceptance. It will help students discover that they are fearfully and wonderfully made in God's image. It will also cause them to take notice that regardless of their skin tone or any other outward feature, they are beautiful just the way they are.

Mirror Activity.

Leaders: Have at least one handheld mirror to pass around so that students can look and see their reflection. Then have each person say one positive thing they see about themselves.

Write down three things that are positive about you. Now, look in the mirror and say something positive about yourself. Example, I am beautiful, smart, talented, and etc.

Song: "As I look in the mirror, what do I see? God's beautiful creation looking back at me."

Read Psalm 139:13-16

For it was You who created my inward parts. You knit me together in my mother's womb. I will praise you because I am remarkably and wonderfully made. Your works are wonderful!

What are your thoughts about yourself?

Are they in alignment with God's thoughts about you?

God is the Potter, we are the clay. He tells us that we are the very works of His hands. In Genesis 1:27 it says, that God created us in his image. He breathed His own breath in each of us and He deemed us good. Who are we to think differently about ourselves? (Romans 9:20) If the Master designer thinks that we are something in which He finds delight and takes pleasure in, we should also embrace His thoughts about who and whose we are.

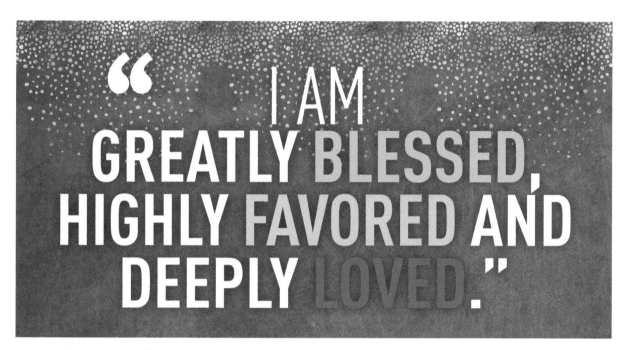

What does God say about me?

He says that:

I am loved—Jeremiah 33:3; Romans 8:38-39; John 3:16

I am Forgiven—1 John 2:12

I am Adopted—Ephesians 1:5

I am complete and whole—Colossians 2:10

I am His—Isaiah 43:1

I am never alone—Joshua 1:9

I am created with purpose—Esther 4:14

I am victorious—I Corinthians 15:57; Romans 8:37

I am beautiful—Psalm 139:13-14

I am worthy—Zephaniah 3:17

I am blessed—Ephesians 1:3

I am an heir—Galatian 4:7

I am His treasure—I Peter 2:9-10

Listen to the Song: "Who You Say I Am" by Hillsong Worship
(https://www.youtube.com/hashtag/whoyousayiam)

Charity Activities.

Self-Esteem Roll

Roll the dice and as you land on the numbers below, respond accordingly.

1. One thing I like about myself
2. A positive message I can say to myself
3. One thing that I am proud that I've done
4. One thing I have done for someone else
5. One thing God says about me
6. Give someone else a compliment

In the book, *Loving the Skin I'm In*, Raven struggles to find acceptance and self-love because she detests her dark skin tone. God sends Charity to help her see that true beauty lies within. Until Raven sees herself through the lens of God, she has a faulty view of her true identity in Christ. Charity helps her to see herself in the very way God sees her and created her to be. In conclusion, she comes to embrace the beauty of her dark skin and begins to see her beauty through God's eyes.

Mirror Activity

Using the mirror image on page 115, write positive affirmations about yourself. These are the things God sees in you.

LESSON 2: LOVING THE SKIN I'M IN

Positive Self-Talk

My Circumstances	God's Word Says
When someone says something mean	I am fearfully and wonderfully made. (*Psalms 139*)
When I feel disappointed	No eye has seen, no ear has heard, nor has it entered the hearts of men the things God has prepared for me. (*1 Corinthians 2:9*)
When I feel frustrated or defeated	I am more than a conqueror. (Romans 8:37)
When I feel I'm not good enough	God loves me with an everlasting love. (*Jeremiah 31:3*)
When I feel embarrassed	If God be for me, who can be against me? (*Romans 8:31*)
When I feel sad or discouraged	—do not fear, God will take care of you. (*Isaiah 41:10*)
When I am afraid or nervous	I can do all things through Christ (*Philippians 4:13*)
When I feel lonely	I will be with you always (*Hebrews 1:6*)

Now that you have discovered what God says about you, what is the one thing that you believe is true about you based on His word?

Charity Application.

When negative thoughts come to your mind, turn your focus toward God and think His thoughts about you. Let your thoughts be guided and dictated by God's word alone.

When others say negative things about you, reflect on the verses listed in this lesson and select one thing you can look in the mirror and say to yourself. Remember, you are fearfully and wonderfully made. Use these affirming words to build yourself and others up and thrive to reflect God's love.

Parent Resource for Building Child's Self-Esteem

Developing Self-Esteem

We can give children the gift of a Christ-centered self-esteem. Here's how:

Let them know how God views them—loved, valued, and esteemed.

Say things such as, "You are special to God" or "The Bible says God loves you so much that he has counted every hair on your head!" We can remind children that God loved them enough to pay the highest price for them—his Son's life.

Celebrate each child's God-given strengths.

When a child displays his or her gifts, point the child to the giver. Say something like, "I thank God for giving you your beautiful voice."

Teach children to persevere.

If a child has difficulty with a problem, don't jump in and save the day. <u>Pray with the child</u> for guidance. Then ask questions to help the child think of solutions. Otherwise, your save-the-day help could send the message that the child isn't capable.

As children grasp that their worth is not rooted in how they perform but in their relationship with God and what God says about them, they'll truly develop positive self-esteem. And their feelings about themselves won't be subject to whether the teacher praises their drawing each time or not.

How to Help Kids Develop a Christ-Centered Self-Esteem

Discover how you can minister to children who have self-esteem issues.

https://childrensministry.com/christ-centered-self-esteem/

Lesson 3
Your Life Matters

Topic: I Matter to God!
Scripture: Proverbs 6:16-19

Memory verse
"...but to do justice, and to love kindness, and to walk humbly with your God" (Micah 6:8 ESV).

Read: *Your Life Matters*

The third lesson will bring awareness to the ongoing problems of injustice in our society. Students will learn how God feels and will understand the importance of treating everyone with love, respect and fairness.

Your Life Matters!

Charity Activities.

Scavenger Hunt

Leaders: Hide these verses around the room and allow the students to find them. Once all verses are found, have the students share their verse.

Psalm 139:13-16	2 Corinthians 12:9
Romans 5:6-8	Luke 12:6-7
Matthew 6:25-31	Genesis 1:27
Jeremiah 29:11	Ephesians 2:10
Ephesians 2:4-9	1 Peter 2:9
Isaiah 43:4	Song of Solomon 4:7
John 3:16	

This book is about a young talented boy who has a bright future. He is athletic and smart. He dreams about being successful and is curious about how the rich lives on the opposite side of his community. One day he decides to venture over to see what it's like. He is captured by a brutal cop and is arrested, until Charity comes on the scene. He then realizes how unjust the law forces are which leads him to take a stand for justice.

There are several biblical examples that come to mind as we deal with the subject of injustice. Among them are Joseph, Moses, Esther, Daniel and the three Hebrew boys. We will revisit their biblical scenarios briefly and observe all the ways in which God intervened to display His love and care.

Leaders: Divide the students into four groups. Give each group one of the biblical characters and have them read the scripture pertaining to each person(s).

Have the students act out the injustice that is prevalent in each scenario. Highlight the response of God to each scene.

Read the following paragraphs about each biblical character prior to the skit being performed.

First, we will look back at the life of Joseph during his prison experience. Prior to him becoming incarcerated he was falsely accused of enticing Potiphar's wife in an undesirable physical affair. As we are aware of the stories' ending, we recognize that Joseph was falsely accused and served an unfair sentence for a crime he did not commit. In the end, God allowed him to be victorious, causing what was designed for evil to bring about his ultimate good.

Next, in the lineup is Moses. Moses was an Israelite, who was raised as an Egyptian. Although he was well-treated by his adoptive family, he witnessed the unjust treatment of his bloodline, the Israelites, being brutally mistreated. Over time, it began to annoy him, which led him to take matters in his hand to deal with the injustice that he observed. Afterwards, he became fearful of what he had done and fled the scene for forty years.

During this time, God did not forget about the Israelites under the rule of Pharoah, because the treatment became more brutal and intense. Eventually God paid a visit to Moses in the wilderness and got his attention through a burning bush. He then appoints Moses to be the leader to set his people free.

Esther was a beautiful young Jewish girl who had been raised by her cousin Mordecai. Out of hundreds of girls in the royal court, Esther had been chosen to be a bride to the King. During this time there was an evil plot being planned by a man named Haman, who was the king's top official. He hated the Jews and wanted them all destroyed. Through Esther's cousin, Mordecai, she found out about Haman's wicked scheme. God used her boldness to make the king aware of the situation so that her people would not be destroyed.

Daniel, along with his three friends, Shadrach, Meshach and Abednego were foreigners who had been taken captive and brought to live in the country of Babylon. While there, they were instructed by the King to follow the traditions of the Babylonians and pledge allegiance to their god. They were loyal to their God, Yahweh and refused to serve the king's foreign god. Consequently, they were thrown into a fiery furnace to be destroyed, however, God stepped in at just the right time to spare their lives.

In all four stories, the outcome is quite miraculous. God was observant to every injustice performed in each of their lives and brought deliverance to his people.

Comprehension Questions.

After reading this story why do you think social injustice still exist in the world?

- **Do you feel that racial inequality still exists today?**

- **What ethnicity groups do you feel receive the worst treatment and why?**

- **What are some examples of racial injustice that have taken place in your lifetime?**

- **What are some things that can be done to make the world a better place to live in unity among ethnic groups?**

- **As Christians, what can we do across racial lines to bring about a change?**

God Cares About Injustice
Scripture: Micah 6:8; Galatians 6:7; 2 Peter 2:9

Genesis—God rescues Joseph from prison

Exodus 13—God leads the children of Israel out of Egypt

Esther—God rescues the Jews from being annihilated by Haman

Daniel—God rescues the Hebrew boys from the burning flames

Charity Activity.

1. Draw a self-portrait and tell why you matter.
2. I matter because . . .

God still operates out of a heart of love and compassion for His people. He continues to hate evil and injustice. Over time He will eventually respond, by awakening society and providing a way of deliverance to right wrongs and bring deliverance to the issues at hand.

Charity Application.

If you are ever treated in an unjust way, maintain your cool. Always cooperate with the law and act in a respectable way. Do your best to make wise decisions and honor God in all that you do. He will do the rest. He says, Vengeance is mine, I will repay. (Romans 12:19)

You are a treasured Black boy, your life is important to me,
I'm shouting from the rooftop for all the world to agree.
You matter when you wake up to see the rising of the day,
And when your rest your head at dawn, when the sky is gray.

You matter when you walk the street or peruse in your car,
regardless of the distance you travel, be it near or far.
You matter if your hair is locked or if it's neatly groomed,
Or if you wear a hoodie, causing others to assume.

You matter if you walk or run alone in the crowded streets,
Or in private communities among the wealthy and elite.
Your life truly matters despite the melanin tone in your skin,
God created you very uniquely with so much purpose within.

I celebrate you amazing Black boy,
your life really matters to me,
I'm shouting from the rooftop for the world to all agree.

Parent Resource for Dealing with Racism

In Genesis 1, God created us and deems us "good"! Who are we to think differently?

A Family Approach to Discussing Racism, Social Injustice, and the Gospel—D6 Family

https://d6family.com/a-family-approach-to-discussing-racism-social-injustice-and-the-gospel

Lesson 4

Sick & Alone

Topic: Dealing With Sickness and Life's Struggles
Scripture: 2 Corinthians 12:6-10; John 4:46-54

Memory verse
"Cast all your anxiety on him because he cares for you" (I Peter 5:7 TNIV).

Read: *Sick & Alone*

This lesson will help children understand that when they suffer from sickness or other issues, God is aware. They will understand that God is compassionate, caring and comforting during their most difficult times.

How many of you have ever been injured or sick? What did your parents do to help you during these times?

Although, they couldn't take your sickness away immediately, they were able to help you feel comforted and comfortable during the pain. All good and loving parents hate to see their children in pain. They do everything in their power to console them until they are completely over the dilemma. They would much rather feel the pain for you, than to see you go through it.

God is also a loving parent, and He does not like to see His loved ones in pain. He may not always take our pain away, but He does bring comfort to us while we are going through our roughest and toughest times.

In John 4, it tells of an event in which Jesus was confronted with a request from a Royal official, whose son was about to die. He asked Jesus if He would come to his house to heal his son. Jesus had compassion on this man and saw his genuine love and concern for his child. He responded, if you believe, your son is already healed. He then told the man to head home.

While the Royal official was on his way home, he saw his servants running towards him. They were coming with the news that his son was healed. The man asked around, about what time did he start to feel better?

They responded and said, it was around the time in which he had spoken to Jesus.

SECTION 2

There are other events in the Bible where Jesus chose to heal others who were sick. In addition, Jesus performed all kinds of miracles so that He could get the people to trust in Him. However, there are situations in which Jesus did not heal. It wasn't because He didn't care, or had the ability to heal; but often, He had a different purpose in mind.

We don't always know why we sometimes must suffer the way we do. One thing is sure, Jesus cares when we do. He is very near to the broken hearted and those who suffer in various ways. He may not take our suffering away, but He tells us that His grace is sufficient to meet us at our point of need. He will bring comfort and peace to get us through our most difficult times. He says to us, Bring all your worries and cares to Him because He cares and is concern about you. (2 Peter 5:7)

In the story, *Sick & Alone*, Charity is sent from Heaven to help a little girl named Natalie, who is terminally ill. This means she has a disease in which she is not going to get better. She is confined to her home and attends school virtually. She misses her friends and doesn't feel like anyone cares about her, or what she is going through. God sends Charity to remind her of His love and care. Through Charity's involvement, she is connected to her friends and becomes fully aware that people really do care.

After reading the story, answer the following questions.

● **Why couldn't Natalie go to school?**

● **How did her friends begin to spend time with her?**

● **What did Charity do to surprise Natalie?**

● **How can you be a friend to someone who is sick and feeling alone?**

Charity Acts.

If you know of a friend who is sick or suffering from any form of illness or disability, be loving, compassionate and caring and do whatever you can to bring a little bit of happiness to their lives.

Song: To the tune of "Ten Little Indians"

Jesus can heal my sick little body, (3xs)
I just need to pray and believe.

He will never leave or forsake me, (3xs)
He will be with me till the end.

I just need to obey and trust Him, (3xs)
No matter what may come my way.

He'll be a friend when everyone forsakes me, (3xs)
Jesus is a forever faithful friend.

Charity Activities.

Jesus and Me poster / Add a picture of you (see section 3, page 88)

Crossword of people Jesus healed (see section 3, page 86)

Lesson 4 Coloring page (see section 3, page 89)

Hidden Images puzzle (see section 3, page 84)

Jesus puzzle (see full size pieces on page 116)

  Materials needed: Scissors, Heavy stock paper, Tape or glue

    Step 1: Cut out the puzzle pieces.
    Step 2: Tape or glue them in the right place.
    Step 3: Write out John 3:16 in the space provided. Insert your name
        where it says, for God so loved (your name)
    Step 4: Commit your special verse to memory

Parent Resources for Sick and Suffering Children

7 Ways Parents Can Help Kids Cope with illness, Joe DiMaggio Children's Hospital (jdch.com)

Lesson 5

A Place to Belong

Topic: I'm in God's Family
Scripture: Exodus 2:1–10

Memory verse
"But to all who did receive Him, He gave them the
right to become children of God" (John 1:12).

Read: *A Place to Belong*

This lesson will help students to see how anyone can be included in the family of
God by simply placing their faith and trust in Him. Also, they will understand how
important it is to reach out to make others feel valued and important.

We are all God's adopted children if we have been reborn into the family of God.

Like Moses, God had a very special purpose for placing him into his adoptive family. He had appointed him from his birth to be instrumental in carrying out His divine plan to deliver His people from bondage. He knew all the details it would take to equip him in carrying forth such a task.

During the time of Moses' birth, the number of Hebrews were being multiplied greatly in Egypt. Pharoah feared that they would become too numerous and take over the land. As a result, he made a law that every male baby had to be tossed into the river to die to keep their numbers from growing out of control.

Moses's mother knew that Moses was special, so instead of following the law, she hid him in a basket near the palace, in hope that he would be found by Pharoah's daughter and spared. This is exactly what happened. One look into the eyes of this special brown eyed adorable baby instantly melted her heart.

Bitiah, Pharoah's daughter, couldn't bring herself to follow her father's orders by putting this Hebrew baby to death. Instead, she decided to adopt the infant and raise him as her own.

As a part of Pharoah's family, Moses shared all the rights and responsible that were associated with being an heir to Pharoah's throne.

God had a purpose in divinely placing Moses into the royal family. He had a plan to use his upbringing as preparation for the role in which he would later use him. His adoption was not a haphazard event, but a divine plan to equip Moses for his mission in leading the Israelites out of bondage. He chose Moses!

God has chosen you and me to be a part of His family. He had a very specific plan in choosing us. He selected us with a divine appointment to carry out His plan. He has also equipped us with what it will take to fulfill His plan for our lives. God has given to each of us specific gifts and talents to carry out His agenda for our lives.

In Ephesians 2:8-10, it says, We are saved by grace through faith, not of ourselves, it is God's doing, His very gift to us so that we should not boast. We are saved to be His workmanship, (masterpiece, or creative design) to carry out His good works, which He prepared for us beforehand, so that we could walk accordingly.

Read each verse and tell what God says about you.

- **Deuteronomy 10:18**
- **Psalm 68: 5-6a**
- **Isaiah 1:17**
- **Isaiah 40:31**

- **Matthew 18:5**
- **Matthew 25:40**
- **James 1:2**

GOD Chose U
John 15:16

This is the fifth story in the Charity Series which tells about a boy named Noah who was placed in foster care. He desperately wanted a family to belong to which was his constant prayer. God sent Charity to unite Noah's heart with his teacher, in whom He had selected to be a perfect match for him. As a result, Noah began to succeed and thrive in ways he had never done before.

When we are positioned with purpose we will thrive and accomplish all that God has created and destined us to be.

Charity Activities.

God's Family Collage Ephesians 1:3-14

Create a poster that tells who is in the family of God and put your picture in the middle. Place each child's picture on a bulletin board and title it, "Adopted by God".

Spiritual Birth Certificates

Create a birth certificate and put the children's spiritual birthdates on it with their handprints. See sample on page 127.

Adoption Party with Cake and Ice Cream

Make or purchase a cake that has all the children's name on it. Title it: God's family.

Have all the children participate in decorating cupcakes. Use a toothpick with a paper attached to write their names. Sing in the tune of Happy birthday, "We've been adopted by God, (three times) We are a part of God's family, we've been adopted by God."

Song: "Father Abraham"

Song: "I'm In the Lord's Army"

Charity Acts.

1. Pray for children without families
2. Become pen pals with kids in foster care/Adopt-a-friend

Parent Resources for Adoption

https://adoption.org/resources-available-help-adoptive-parents

Lesson 6
Trouble at Home

Topic: Abuse, Handle with Care
Scripture: Ephesians 4:32

Memory verse

"But Jesus said, 'Let the little children come to me and do not hinder them, for to such belongs the kingdom of heaven'" (Matthew 19:14 TNIV).

Read: *Trouble at Home*

Students will recognize the importance of godly discipline and how important it is for their growth and development. However, they will also learn how God desires all parents to follow His guidelines and not act out of control.

This story is about a family that appears to have everything good occurring on the outside, but trouble is brewing on the inside. They give a pretentious view that everything is ok, but their lives are filled with chaos. Everything begins to unravel when the dad's drinking gets out of control. Abuse then takes place in the home. This leaves the children misplaced and very sadden because they are now without their parents.

Opening Song: "Jesus Loves the Little Children"

Comprehension Questions.

After reading the story, answer each question.

- **Why were the children separated from their parents?**

- **What did Charity do to bring peace back into their home?**

- **If there is trouble in your home, what would you do?**

"Be kind to one another, tenderhearted, forgiving one another, as God in Christ forgave you" (Ephesians 4:32 ESV).

What does the Bible say about Abuse?

Read the following scriptures.

How should parents treat their children?

Proverbs 19:18; Ephesians 6:4; Colossians 3:21; Proverbs 13:24; Proverbs 22:15; Ephesians 6:4; Proverbs 22:6

What leads to abuse?

Proverbs 14:29; James 1:20-21; Proverbs 29:22; Proverbs 19:19; Proverbs 22:24

Self-Control can prevent abuse

Proverbs 16:29

Abusers will have to answer to God

Mark 9:42; Galatians 5:20-21; Ephesians 4:26

God will restore healing to the abused

Psalm 147:3

How Parents Should Treat Their Children

Proverbs 19:18

<u>Discipline</u> your son while there is hope; don't set your heart on being the cause of his death.

Ephesians 6:4

Fathers, don't stir up anger in your children, but bring them up in the <u>training and instruction of the Lord</u>

Colossians 3:21

Fathers, <u>do not exasperate your children</u>, so that they won't become discouraged.

Proverbs 13:24

The one who will not <u>use the rod</u> hates his son, but the one who loves him disciplines him diligently.

Proverbs 22:15

Foolishness is bound to the heart of a youth; <u>a rod of discipline</u> will separate it from him.

Proverbs 22:6

<u>Start a youth out</u> on his way; even when he grows old he will not depart from it. (CSV)

What Leads to Abuse

Proverbs 14:29

A patient person shows great understanding, but a <u>quick-tempered</u> one promotes foolishness.

James 1:20-21

. . . for human <u>anger</u> does not accomplish God's righteousness. Therefore, ridding yourselves of all <u>moral filth</u> and the <u>evil</u> that is so prevalent, humbly receive the implanted word, which is able to save your souls.

Proverbs 29:22

An <u>angry</u> person stirs up conflict, and a <u>hot-tempered</u> one increases rebellion.

Proverbs 19:19

A person with <u>intense anger</u> bears the penalty; if you rescue him, you'll have to do it again.

Proverbs 22:24

Don't make friends with an <u>angry</u> person, and don't be a companion of a hot-tempered one.

Do Not Turn Your Children's Heart Away from God

Proverbs 16:29

A violent person lures his neighbor, leading him on a path that is not good.

Mark 9:42

"But whoever causes one of these little ones who believe in me to fall away—it would be better for him if a heavy millstone were hung around his neck and he were thrown into the sea."

Galatians 5:20-21

. . . idolatry, sorcery, hatreds, strife, jealousy, outbursts of anger, selfish ambitions, dissensions, factions, envy, drunkenness, carousing, and anything similar. I am warning you about these things—as I warned you before—that those who practice such things will not inherit the kingdom of God.

Song: "Because of Whose I Am", Lyrics by Wayne Watson (verse 1 and chorus)

I'll never understand
Why He saw a piece of clay
And said, "I want it, I'll use it."

The greatest mystery
Is somehow in spite of me
He said, "I'm gonna love you."

He took me in His arms
Said, "This child belongs to me."
He placed me in His Kingdom
Now I live like royalty

It's not because of what I am
Not because of what I've done
But because of Whose I am.

Charity Acts.

Be kind in your actions towards others. If you or someone you know is being abused, do not keep it to yourself, but make it known to a trusting adult, Trust them to seek out help and provide the necessary interventions to change the situation.

Charity Activities.

Emotional Wheel

When you are experiencing feelings and you need to identify how you feel, use the emotions wheel. (see section 3, page 118)

Leaders: Practice coming up with different scenarios to help children sort through and identify their feelings.

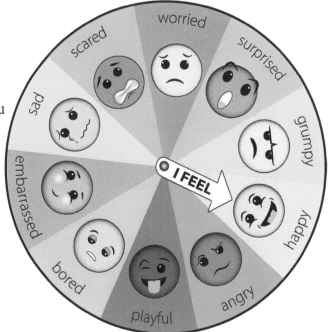

Self-Control Remote

10 Self-Control Games

10 Awesome Games to Teach Kids Self Control in School Counseling (counselorkeri.com)

Parent Resources for Abuse

Resources for Identifying, Preventing, and Responding to Abuse

Anglican Diocese of the Upper Midwest (midwestanglican.org) https://midwestanglican. org/resources-for-identifying-preventing-and-responding-to-abuse

Lesson 7

Don't Bully Me!

Topic: Kindness always win!
Scripture: Ephesians 4:32

Memory verse
"If God is for us, who can be against us? He who did not spare his own Son but gave him up for us all. How will He not also with Him grant us everything?" (Romans 8:32).

Read: *Don't Bully Me!*

Students will understand what bullying looks like and the importance of speaking up and out against it, if they are ever confronted by a bully.

Definition of Bullying[1]

adjective

prone to or characterized by overbearing mistreatment and domination of others

Opening—Is this Bullying Activity? (Pinterest)

Leaders: Have the children answer these questions and give examples if they are willing to do so.

1. Have you ever been bullied?
2. Have you ever bullied anyone?
3. Why do people bully others?
4. What would you do if you were ever bullied?

Teasing	Conflict
• Everyone is having fun	• No one is having fun
• No one is getting hurt physically or mentally	• There is a possible solution
• Everyone is participating equally to the disagreement	• Equal balance of power
Mean Moment	**Bullying**
• Someone is being hurt on purpose either physically or mentally	• Someone is being mean on purpose
• Reaction to a strong feeling or emotion	• Repetitive (happens regularly)
• An isolated event (doesn't happen regularly)	• Imbalance of power

Scripture:

Daniel 5:3–4

Daniel was bullied by the king's royal officials because he refused to follow the King's decree not to pray to his God.

1   https://www.merriam-webster.com/dictionary/bullying

Esther 7:1-3
Esther's cousin Mordecai was bullied by Haman because he hated the Jews.

Jesus (the four gospels, Matthew, Mark, Luke, and John) Jesus constantly had bullies who tried to set Him up and find flaws in Him. They even had Him arrested, beaten, and killed.

> Bullies don't want others pointing out their flaws or imperfections; they want to be in charge.

If you are bullied, Jesus knows what you are going through. He experienced the loneliness and pain associated with being bullied Himself.

Read 2 Timothy 1:17 Do not be afraid to speak up and out to make it known.

Is It Bullying?

When someone says or does something unintentionally hurtful and they do it only once.

That's Rude

When someone says or does something intentionally hurful and they do it only once.

That's Mean

When someone says or does something intentionally hurtful and they keep doing it even when you tell them to stop, or show them that you're upset.

That's Bullying!

Charity Acts.

Be on the lookout for anyone in your social setting who is being bullied or mistreated. Speak up and out, when it's safe, against the bully's actions. Talk to a trusted friend or adult and seek out help for the person in need.

Charity Activities.

Use the chart to create scenarios about when and how to act when confronted with a bully. For example, if you see a bully calling your friend cruel names, what should you do? (For full sized wheel, see section 3, page 119)

Parent Resource for Bullying

(For full size chart and character set see page page 120.)

www.SuccessinLearning.net

1. Stand up straight and say, "Leave me alone!"
2. Hold your hand out and say, "Stop it!"
3. Move away to a crowded area.
4. Talk to a teacher, parent, or friend.
5. Stay calm, talk friendly.

https://familyfire.com/articles/bullying-a-christian-perspective-and-response

Bullying: A Christian Perspective and Response

https://familyfire.com/articles/bullying-a-christian-perspective-and-response

Lesson 8

The Easter Story

Topic: Jesus Saves
Scripture: Matthew 27-28

Read: *The Easter Story*

Students will understand the significance of the birth, death, and resurrection of our Savior and how they can come to know Him personally.

Do you really know what Easter is all about?

Why did Jesus really have to die?

What does the Easter story reveal about the heart of God?

Each of these questions will be answered through our study today.

In the beginning of creation, God chose to make man. He loved what He had created. He created man in his very image. He wanted to have a close relationship with him.

After God made man, He made him a companion called woman which he used man's rib to create. He later set up a place for them to live. He then showed them trees in the garden where they could freely eat. He also gave them instructions on what not to eat. Every tree was good, except one. God specifically told them not to eat from only one tree.

Has there ever been a time in your life in which you were told not to do something and you did it anyway? What happened because of your disobedience?

The Easter Story—Our Disobedience

In Romans 3:23 it tells us that all have sinned and come short of the glory of God.

Man's disobedience led to our sinful nature. The word sin means, we fell out of grace with God. This brought a distance in our relationship with Him. God could no longer befriend man and hang out with him. There was a gap.

This meant that man and God were completely separated by sin.

In Romans 6:23, it says that the wages of sin is death. We were spiritually separated from God. There was nothing we could do to close the gap.

In Romans 5:8 it says that God demonstrates His own love for us in this: While we were sinners, Christ died for us.

In essence, Jesus is God's provision to take care of our sins once and for all. We couldn't do anything to bridge the gap, but God could, and He did. He gave us His Son, Jesus, to die on the cross, so that our sins could be forgiven. Jesus' death was the bridge needed to pave the gap and to settle our account with God.

He Has Risen So We Are Forgiven

The Easter Story reminds us of what took place on the cross to deal with our sins. We are forgiven because, not only did Jesus die on the cross, but three days later, He rose. Yes, He came back to life. He died and then rose again to let us know that He was able to pay the debt that we owed. He was also victorious in closing the gap so that we could enjoy a relationship with God once again.

We celebrate this important day, because He rose, we have been pardoned and no longer owe a price we could not pay. We celebrate Easter because the blood of Jesus washed our sins away. We celebrate Easter because we are no longer destined to hell, but we can live with Jesus in Heaven forever more.

Charity Activity.

Use musical instruments to have a victory party to celebrate the victorious resurrection of Jesus.

Write a letter or draw a card to express your gratitude to God for sending His Son Jesus.

If you have not accepted Jesus in your life, just repent of your sins and ask Him into your heart.

Use "Resurrection Eggs" as a way to visually communicate the events of Easter.

Charity Acts.

If you have never invited Jesus into your heart, you can do it right now. Simply agree with God that you are a sinner and need Him to forgive you. Agree to live for Him, accept his forgiveness, and whole-heartedly commit to following Him.

If you have accepted him in your heart, share Jesus' love with someone who has not decided to follow Him.

Parent Resource for Sharing God's Love with Your Child

If you haven't already, read *Charity Presents The Easter Story*.

Lesson 9

Mom's My Shero!

Topic: Honor Your Mom

Scripture: Proverbs 31

Read: *Mom's My Shero!*

Students will understand the value and significant role of a mother and how she is to be respected and honored when she lives a life that is pleasing to God.

Mothers are a Kiss from God.

It may or may not be Mother's Day, but everyday is a reason to celebrate mothers.

- **What are some of the characteristics listed about the woman in Proverbs 31?**

- **What are some things that you read that are characteristic of your mom?**

- **What is the one thing you admire and appreciate the most about your mom?**

- **Who are some of the women in your life that remind you of the lady in Proverbs 31?**

Describe something special your mother has done for you.

Share about a time your mother was sad and in need of a God-encounter?

Comprehension Questions.

After reading *Mom's My Shero!* answer the following questions.

Why caused the mom to have to struggle?

What did Charity do to the mom to help her get through her hard times?

What can you do to help your mom when she becomes overwhelmed with life?

The Virtuous Woman
by Stephanie A. Kilgore-White

In Proverbs 31 we see,
the image of the woman we want to be,
Who is both the mother and the wife,
serving, living, loving life.

She rises at the break of day,
to conquer the world without delay,
Her priorities and duties are all intact,
she looks first to God and that's a fact.

To gain knowledge wisdom and true insight,
so that she might serve with all her might,
Her husband and children are given care,
then off she goes to handle her affair.

She's adorned with beauty,
from the inside out,
and the world takes notice,
as she goes about.

Her desire is to leave a visible print,
and the fragrance of her god-scent,
She reveres her God and serves him vehemently,
and honors and serves him oh so diligently.

All who knows her sings her praises so sweet,
as her family applauds and sits at her feet,
To revere a woman who serves her King,
with whom she adores and whose praises she brings.

Charity Activities.

Mom it's your day!
Proverbs 31:31 TNIV

"Honor her for all that her hands have done, and let her works bring her praise at the city gate."

Make a coupon book with five ways you plan to help your mom out. For example:

1. Wash the dishes (for a week).
2. Sweep the floor.
3. Run her a bubble bath.
4. Decorate a crown and present it to your mom.
5. Make a card to let your mom know how much you appreciate her.
6. Do something without being asked.
7. Make her breakfast in bed (if you are old enough).

Charity Acts.

Acknowledge to your mom all the things you appreciate about her and honor her for being the God appointed queen in your family. Always show her respect and demonstrate obedience to her instructions.

Single Mom Guide to Raising Godly Kids Resource

Raising a godly family as a single mom

Focus on the Family.ca/content/ raising-a-godly-family-as-a-single-mom

Lesson 10

Where's My Dad?

Topic: God is a good, good father!
Scripture: 1 Timothy 5:8

Memory verse
"And my God will supply every need of yours according to his riches and glory in Christ Jesus" (Philippians 4:19).

Read: *Where's My Dad?*

Students will understand how important it is to value their father's presence in their lives. On the contrary, if dad isn't present, they will learn the significance of having God provide fulfilment in His role as their Heavenly Father.

LESSON 10: WHERE'S MY DAD

Song: "Oh where oh where has my daddy gone, oh where, oh where can he be? He has not been here for my family, oh where oh where can he be?"

According to the U.S. Census, in 2020 there were more than 18.6 million children in America living with one parent. Among that number 15.3 million or 21% live without a dad in the home.[1]

How many of you have your dad living in your home?

How many of you know of other kids your age whose dad is missing from the home?

Growing up without a father is quite difficult. Every little girl desires to have a daddy to give her hugs, and to express positive feelings towards her. Without the presence of a loving dad, many girls struggle with a healthy self-esteem.

Every boy longs to have a dad to toss a ball, wrestle, and exert his ability to showcase his strength. When a child's dad is not around it leaves a void and can cause confusion about gender roles.

God created the role of a dad to provide safety and security to his family. He also intended for the dad to be the provider, to care for the family's needs. When a dad is not present, the family often lacks the resources that are needed, which may lead to poverty and other unfortunate outcomes.

God never intended for families to be without the presence of a dad. It was and still is His desire for every boy and girl to grow up with a father in their lives. However, due to sin and the fall of man, this is not the case for so many children.

---

1 Hemez, Paul, and Chanell Washington "Number of Children Living Only With Their Mothers Has Doubled in Past 50 Years." US Census Bureau. "Resource Library." census.gov. Apr 12, 2021. https://www.census.gov/library/stories/2021/04/number-of-children-living-only-with-their-mothers-has-doubled-in-past-50-years.html.

As a result, God desires to be present in the lives of His children so that they can find the comfort and security that only He can bring.

Unlike the missing dad, God will never leave His children, nor will he ever abandon them. He promises to be right there to meet a child's every need. He is a perfect, loving Father!

Where's My Dad? is about a boy name Khalil who starts off in life with his father. Over time due to constant conflict in the home, the father decides to abandon the home, leaving him without his dad.

Due to the confusion of the father being missing from the home, Khalil begins to act out in school. His performance, both academically and behaviorally, takes a turn for the worst. His mom is concerned and calls on God for help.

- **How would you feel if your dad was no longer present in your life?**

- **How do you feel about your dad not being around and involved in your life?**

- **How would your life be different if he was present in your home?**

- **Do you think you would behave differently if your circumstances changed?**

- **How does knowing God as your father affect your attitude or situation?**

God, Our Father

Psalm 18:30—He is a faithful Father who does no wrong. Everything that he does is upright and pure (perfect).

Psalm 68:5—He will be a father to the fatherless.

Isaiah 64:8—He is the Potter, we are the clay and the very work of His hand.

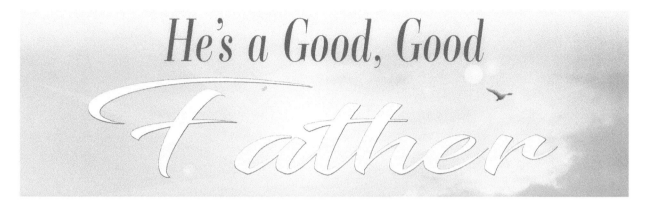

He's a Good, Good Father

1 John 3:1—God has a great love towards his children.

2 Corinthians 6:18—God promises to be a loving, caring and nurturing father to those who are his children.

God, the Perfect Father

God delights in providing for the needs of His children. He says in Psalm 84:11, no good thing will He withhold from us, if we walk according to His ways.

For the LORD God is a sun and shield. The LORD grants favor and honor; He does not withhold the good from those who live with integrity.

Philippians 4:19—He promises to provide for all of our needs according to His riches and glory.

Jeremiah 31:3—God's love for his children is incomprehensible. He says He loves us with an everlasting love.

Romans 8:38–39—His love can never be interrupted, nor will it ever pause, no matter what we experience in this life. He loves us and that will never ever change.

"For I am convinced that neither death nor life, neither angels nor demons, neither the present nor the future, nor any powers, neither height nor depth, nor anything else in all creation, will be able to separate us from the love of God that is in Christ Jesus our Lord" (Romans 8:38–39 TNIV).

Charity Acts.

Develop a relationship with your Heavenly Father and trust Him to be there for you. Ask God to provide you with a father-figure whom you can trust to also be present in your life.

Allow God's word to give you guidance, comfort, and security that only a Father can guarantee.

Song: "You're A Good, Good Father" (https://youtu.be/CqybaIesbuA)
Song: "Father Abraham" (https://youtu.be/DPKp4AWmQoI)

Charity Activity.

1. Make Father's Day Cards for God
2. Make a Prayer Cube
   (see page 125)
3. Make a Prayer Bookmark
4. Color the sheet on page 111

Teach the Lord's Prayer

Matthew 6:9–15

What it really means:[2]

God,
God is with us on Earth too,
But He is especially in Heaven,
To remind us to use God's name respectfully,
Especially when we pray to Him.

Our Father,
Who art in Heaven,
Hallowed be Thy name.

Thy kingdom come,
Thy will be done,
On earth as it is in heaven.

Give us this day our
daily bread,
And forgive our trespasses,
As we forgiven those who
trespass against us.

Lead us not into temptation,
But deliver us from evil.

But if you donot forgive
others their sins,
Your Father will not forgive
your sins. Amen.

---

2 http://2.bp.blogspot.com/-jYoV55bNMeE/VDiMGJyJOiI/AAAAAAAAAWE/8APRjZuaoF0/s1600/Our%2BFather%2Bexplanation.jpg

We ask God to share some blessings of Heaven with us,
While we follow His plans for us on Earth,
Just like the saints and angles follow His plans in Heaven.

"Daily bread" is a way of saying what we absolutely need,
And forgive us in the same way we forgive each other.

Help us not to be tempted,
And protect us from any evil.

Amen means "I believe".

Parent Resource for the Absentee Father

Kate Anthony

(https://kateanthony.com/how-to-talk-to-your-son-about-his-absent-father/)

Raising a godly family as a single mom—Focus on the Family

(https://www.focusonthefamily.ca/content/raising-a-godly-family-as-a-single-mom)

7 Encouraging Bible Verses For The Single Mom

(https://www.whatchristianswanttoknow.com/7-encouraging-bible-verses-for-the-single-mom/)

Lesson 11

Heaven Couldn't Wait

Topic: What Awaits Us in Heaven
Scripture: Revelations 21:1-4 CBS

Memory verse
"In fact, we are confident, and we would prefer to be away from the body and at home with the Lord" (2 Corinthians 5:8).

Read: *Heaven Couldn't Waiit*

Students will get a glimpse of heaven from scripture and see that it is a desirable place. They will also come to understand that losing a loved one is painful, but also a place that God has prepared for those He love.

LESSON 11: HEAVEN COULDN'T WAIT

Then I saw a new heaven and a new earth; for the first heaven and the first earth had passed away, and the sea was no more. I also saw the holy city, the new Jerusalem, coming down out of heaven from God, prepared like a bride adorned for her husband.

Then I heard a loud voice from the throne: Look, God's dwelling is with humanity, and he will live with them. They will be his peoples, and God himself will be with them and will be their God. He will wipe away every tear from their eyes. Death will be no more; grief, crying, and pain will be no more, because the previous things have passed away.

Read full chapter[1]

Scripture: 2 Corinthians 5:8
In fact, we are confident, and we would prefer to be away from the body and at home with the Lord.

Today's topic may be difficult to discuss. It is never easy to say goodbye to a loved one or see someone suffer with a terminal illness. We even have a harder time if it is someone that we hold extremely dear to us, like a parent, grandparent, sibling or close friend.

The bible has a lot to say about this subject, especially since Jesus experienced this Himself while on earth. Even though, He had the power to heal, this was not always God's plan. There are times that God will heal, but then other times that God desires to take a loved one home to heaven. Because He is a loving Father, He knows what is best.

---

1   https://www.biblegateway.com/passage/?search=Revelation+21&version=CSB

Often, Jesus will deliver a person from pain and misery by allowing their life to end on this side. It's not because He doesn't care about the family, but He cares more about the individual that is suffering. He wants to deliver them from the pain and set them free.

During these times, we hurt because we want to cling to the person that is so dear to us. Always remember that Jesus loves them even more. We grieve and often sorrow because this is such a difficult pill to swallow. However, we can find comfort in the God who sees our sorrow because He cares immensely for us. In 1 Peter 5:7, it says for us to give all our worries and cares to God because He cares for us.

Jesus Heals:

- **The royal official's son**

- **The paralytic man**

- **Lazarus**

There are numerous occasions throughout the Bible where God is given the credit for healing people physically. He is known as Jehovah-Rapha, the God who heals. He can heal and He does heal, however there are times that He has a different plan in mind. We may not understand or agree with what He decides. Despite our ability to understand, we need to remember that God is a loving Father, who cares deeply about His children, both the sick and the suffering and those who experience loss and grief. He cares!

He cares for those who are sick and suffering and chooses death as a way to relieve them and end the trials of their painful experience. He knows that living is so much better in the life to come, which guarantees no suffering or pain. He ends their misery and takes them to live in Heaven, pain-free for the rest of their lives

God's Abiding Care and Comfort During Grief[2]

> **READ EACH VERSE AND SHARE HOW GOD'S LOVE IS DEMONSTRATED.**
>
> • I am always with you. Psalm 73:23, NIV
>
> • God will wipe away every tear. Revelation 21:4, NKJV
>
> • I am the Lord your God. I am holding your right hand. Isaiah 41:13, ICB
>
> • You will feel safe because there is hope. Job 11:18, ICB
>
> • He heals the broken-hearted. Psalm 147:3, NKJV
>
> • The last enemy to be destroyed is death. 1 Corinthians 15:26, ESV
>
> • The Lord is my helper; I will not be afraid. Hebrews 13:6, NIV
>
> • God will yet fill your mouth with laughter. Job 8:21, ICB

We will all have to journey down the path to death one day. The bible says in Hebrews 9:27, And as it is appointed unto us once to die, but after this the judgment. We are not aware of when and how it will happen, but we know that it will. The Bible tells us in John 3:16, that God so loved each of us that He gave His only begotten Son, Jesus, so that when we die, we will not perish, but would have everlasting life.

This life that He promises is eternal, which means it is a life that will never end. It is a life where there will be joy, unspeakable joy. It's a life in which we will always be happy forevermore as we dwell in the presence of God and all His beloved children.

---

2   https://www.kathleenfucciministries.org/blog/8-verses-for-a-grieving-child

It is promised to be a life that will have a true fairy-tale ending with a "happy-ever-after" reality.

Charity Acts.

When you begin to feel sad and upset about missing your loved one, hold on to the happy memories and talk to God about them. He will bring you comfort during these times.

Charity Craft.

Creating Mansions

MATERIAL NEEDED:
Gold Glitter
Silver Glitter
Gold and Silver Sharpies
Jewels and Rhinestones
Cartons (Milk–big and small)

Song: I Can Only Imagine by Tamela Mann[3]

Parent Resource: Teaching Children About Heaven

DLTK's Bible Stories for Children

Heaven[4]

by Sharla Guenther

Have you ever wondered about heaven? Where is it? What it's like? Who lives there? The Bible talks a bit about heaven and God has given us some hints about what it will be like. However, a lot of it is still a mystery to us because God is still preparing a place for us. At least that's what Jesus told his disciples before he went up to heaven.

---

3   https://www.youtube.com/watch?v=-s8HMmvN-Jc
4   https://www.dltk-kids.com/bible/cv/heaven.htm

LESSON 11: HEAVEN COULDN'T WAIT

He said He was preparing a place for us with many rooms or mansions. Which makes me think that if God created the world and everything in and around it in six days, how amazing will heaven be if He's taking longer than that? If you can think of a beautiful mountain, waterfall or even the prettiest flower you've ever seen and think of a place even more amazing than that, I think that's what heaven will be like.

God can use whatever He wants gold, diamonds and amazing things we haven't even seen on earth. Maybe that's why the Bible doesn't give us a complete description of heaven because we wouldn't even be able to understand how amazing and beautiful it really is.

We can talk more about what heaven is like later. First we should talk about how we can get to heaven and what are some ways we can prepare to go there. Don't worry you don't need to pack a suitcase. In fact, God specifically says that we shouldn't spend all our time on earth trying to collect a bunch of things because we can't take any of it with us.

It might seem strange that we won't need any of our things like our favorite doll or toy truck or even a change of underwear!! God will give us everything we need plus much more. We won't even be bored in heaven because God knows what we need and He's getting it all ready for us.

We still haven't answered the question about how we get to heaven. Actually one of Jesus' disciples named Thomas asked Jesus: We don't know where you're going, so how can we know the way? (John 14:5) Jesus answered: I am the way, the truth and the life no one comes to the Father except through me. This might sound like strange directions but what Jesus was saying is that if you believe the Bible and believe that Jesus died and rose again for you, then you believe in the truth and He will bring you to Heaven.

Not only that, the words God tells us in the Bible will help us in life right now and are like a map that will lead us on the right path and then eventually to Heaven. For example Jesus says that by helping others by feeding them if they're hungry, visiting the sick, giving clothes to those who don't have much, and even by visiting people in jail or who have done things that are wrong. When we do these things it's like we're doing it for Him. (Matthew 25:31-46)

By helping others now, God will give us a reward in heaven. (Matthew 5:12) One of these rewards is a crown. The Bible says that the Lord will reward each person a crown of righteousness when we get there. Imagine your very own crown!

The best part of all is what heaven will be like. Most of this is written in the last two chapters of the Bible. It says that God will wipe every tear from our eyes and there will be no more death, sadness, crying or pain. Everything will be made new again! You won't be able to get hurt anymore and there won't be any fighting or hitting or crying EVER! That sounds pretty neat.

It also says that there won't be a church or temple there because the Lord God Almighty and Jesus are the church. Instead of going to church to learn and worship God we just can go right to Him.

LESSON 11: HEAVEN COULDN'T WAIT

The city of heaven won't need a sun, moon or lights because God's glory will give light to everything. Plus there will be no night time there (I think that means no more naptime or sleeping)! It gets better! Nothing bad will ever enter heaven either.

The Bible tells us a little about what it will look like. It talks in Revelation about the city walls and how they are decorated with precious stones. The wall will be made of pure gold and then 12 different kinds of beautiful stones will cover and decorate it. Some of these stones we don't even know about on earth and other stones we wear in rings and necklaces and are worth a lot of money.

There will be twelve gates and each one will be made of one humungous pearl bigger than you! On top of that, the streets will be made of gold! I can't even imagine how amazing it will be. No dirt or dust just shiny beautiful streets and walls filled with different colored stones reflecting the light from God.

The only tricky part before we get to heaven is how we move from this world to this amazing place. If we believe God, that He died and rose again, need his forgiveness and try to live the way God wants; then God writes our name in the book of life. (Philippians 4:3) Everyone who believes and accepts Jesus will go to heaven and live forever there.

Then there are two ways we can move to heaven. The first way is if we die and the second way is when Jesus comes again while we're alive on earth. The thought of death can be scary (for grown-ups too) BUT, if we keep reminding ourselves how great heaven is maybe it wouldn't have to be so scary.

That second way we can go to Heaven is called the second coming. When God decides it's time for everyone who believes in Him to come to heaven He is going to come get us. It says in the Bible that nobody will ever know when this will be and He will come and we'll all know and see Jesus. There will be angels and trumpets and it'll be very exciting for all those who believe.

As you can see, heaven is going to be a big party and a fabulous place to be with God who made us and wants to reward us. God loves us even more than our parents and promises to take the best care of us. He hasn't forgot us either, He says three times in the last chapter of the Bible that Jesus is coming soon and to keep doing what is right and holy.

Section

In this section there are various activities (puzzles, cryptograms, Wordsearch, coloring sheets and visual charts) that will serve to engage the students and cause them to connect more fully to the lessons.

Charity Activty Sheets.

Hidden Images

Find the 20 hearts hidden in the coloring page below.

Lesson 1 Activities

Cryptoquote Challenge

Fill in each blank with the corresponding letter that matches the number to reveal the hidden message.

$$\overline{} \quad \overline{}\ \overline{} \quad \overline{} \qquad \overline{}\ \overline{}\ \overline{}\ \overline{}\ \overline{}\ \overline{} \qquad \overline{}\ \overline{}$$

9   1 13   1   6 18 9 5 14 4   15 6

$$\overline{}\ \overline{}\ \overline{}\ .$$

7 15   4

KEY

A-1	F-6	K-11	P-16	U-21	Z-26
B-2	G-7	L-12	Q-17	V-22	
C-3	H-8	M-13	R-18	W-23	
D-4	I-9	N-14	S-19	X-24	
E-5	J-10	O-15	T-20	Y-25	

Word Search Challenge

Words can be found in any direction (including diagonals) and can overlap each other. Use the word bank below each challenge.

P	M	L	R	O	B	Z	S	Z	H	S	S	E	L	F	L	E	S	M	I
R	T	D	E	P	E	N	D	A	B	L	E	V	Z	T	N	L	U	T	U
C	M	G	N	O	L	E	F	I	L	A	S	R	A	C	G	J	N	R	G
I	T	Q	A	R	O	B	H	G	I	E	N	L	F	C	G	W	X	U	H
T	G	Y	O	F	B	I	D	B	Z	M	L	X	A	O	N	A	M	S	V
E	N	P	M	D	V	D	S	D	Y	Y	A	R	I	M	I	F	E	T	C
H	I	F	V	W	C	O	R	D	I	A	L	D	T	P	V	F	I	W	F
T	T	F	R	I	E	N	D	S	H	I	P	R	H	A	I	E	N	O	M
A	S	Y	R	Z	W	K	J	W	N	R	L	B	F	S	G	C	T	R	D
P	A	N	S	H	I	D	G	Z	H	G	O	L	U	S	R	T	I	T	U
M	L	H	E	A	R	T	F	E	L	T	N	M	L	I	O	I	M	H	E
E	J	O	N	A	T	H	A	N	C	Q	K	I	P	O	F	O	A	Y	S
Q	I	S	T	L	B	M	J	D	N	I	K	X	R	N	O	N	T	Z	O
K	M	L	N	A	L	R	N	E	I	U	Q	O	V	A	N	A	E	H	L
Q	L	T	K	X	L	U	O	M	R	K	L	U	W	T	C	T	X	N	C
V	G	Y	L	O	F	P	D	T	Q	F	P	P	A	E	D	E	I	N	Z
X	E	Z	Y	C	K	K	I	Q	H	E	G	N	I	V	O	L	R	E	O
Q	Q	A	U	H	A	K	V	M	P	E	S	R	F	R	I	E	N	D	K
H	L	U	X	Q	H	P	A	I	W	S	R	S	U	H	H	G	C	E	C
W	O	E	C	H	U	J	D	C	S	I	S	T	E	R	H	V	A	A	X

Word Bank

1. Jonathan
2. kind
3. David
4. loving
5. selfless
6. close
7. empathetic
8. fun
9. caring
10. loyal
11. dependable
12. ally
13. forgiving
14. friendship
15. cordial
16. brother
17. sister
18. intimate
19. faithful
20. friend
21. affectionate
22. heartfelt
23. neighbor
24. lifelong
25. lasting
26. trustworthy
27. compassionate

Crossword

Word Bank

Charity	Lonely	Prayer
Depart	Love	Special
Downtrodden	Mission	Steam
Example	Outcast	Unconditional
Friendship	Possibilities	Unique

Across

4. Motivation or drive to do something daring

6. Down on one's luck or good fortune

10. Without limits or conditions

12. One of a kind

13. A strong bond with another person

15. Unique

Down

1. One's ultimate life assignment

2. To leave or withdraw

3. A deep emotional feeling

5. Chance or opportunity to make something happen

7. Communication with God

8. all alone, in need of a friend

9. Left out and alone

11. Heart shaped character in the series

14. A demonstration

Coloring Page

Lesson 2 Activities

Cryptoquote Challenge

Fill in each blank with the corresponding letter that matches the number to reveal the hidden message.

9		1	13		6	5	1	18	6	21	12	12	25		1	14	4

23	15	14	4	5	18	6	21	12	12	25		13	1	4	5	.

KEY

A-1	F-6	K-11	P-16	U-21	Z-26
B-2	G-7	L-12	Q-17	V-22	
C-3	H-8	M-13	R-18	W-23	
D-4	I-9	N-14	S-19	X-24	
E-5	J-10	O-15	T-20	Y-25	

Math Challenge

Using the answers from the Math Challenge below as your key. Fill in each blank with the corresponding letter to match the number to see the message.

1)   50/5 + 10/2 + 2 X 5 = _____

2)   4/2 x 7 + 1 = _____

3)   (3)^2 X 2 + 3 = _____

4)   (40/8) + (20/4) /2 = _____

5)   (48/12)/2 + (24 /12) = _____

6)   100/25 x 9/3 + (42/7) = _____

7)   (6 x 6) / (3 X 2) + (4 X 1) + 2 = _____

8)   (3 X 7) + ((2 − 1) /1) = _____

9)   (10/5) /(6/3) + 0 = _____

$$\underline{}\ \underline{}\ \underline{}\quad \underline{}\ \underline{}\ \underline{}\quad \underline{}\ \underline{}\ \underline{}\ \underline{}\ \underline{}\ !$$
  25   15   21   1   18   5   12   15   22   5   4

Word Search Challenge

Words can be found in any direction (including diagonals) and can overlap each other. Use the word bank below each challenge.

E	H	K	B	L	E	S	S	E	D	U	B	W	L	H	R	C	U	K	C
W	Z	W	O	U	K	W	R	O	Y	A	L	S	A	D	O	P	T	E	D
I	N	F	E	R	J	L	X	S	D	B	Q	H	M	V	Z	Z	N	C	E
T	N	R	L	I	C	I	T	E	L	A	I	C	E	P	S	X	O	R	T
G	R	T	C	E	R	B	D	Z	E	G	I	R	X	I	D	M	X	D	R
X	I	W	E	H	D	U	S	V	M	L	B	A	C	B	P	G	E	N	A
S	W	F	K	L	Z	Z	C	F	I	C	P	D	U	L	I	R	Z	C	M
X	I	S	T	Y	L	A	H	O	S	C	Y	M	E	O	U	Y	C	R	S
J	Q	P	R	E	C	I	O	U	S	T	T	T	E	S	T	M	A	E	Z
Q	L	Z	Y	B	D	O	G	W	R	U	E	O	A	T	I	R	N	A	D
T	O	C	M	C	X	C	C	E	L	C	O	E	R	Z	V	K	K	T	E
L	V	B	M	Z	H	X	A	U	N	Z	R	G	I	I	M	Y	X	I	N
L	E	S	S	E	V	O	F	P	N	T	I	O	H	R	O	P	O	O	I
L	D	Z	E	R	G	R	S	E	A	W	O	R	T	H	Y	U	W	N	M
O	A	P	Q	E	E	H	V	E	R	B	Q	E	H	J	N	D	S	A	R
I	K	Z	Z	D	N	I	O	I	N	E	L	B	A	R	O	N	O	H	E
Y	A	W	N	C	G	G	D	S	N	T	D	E	T	F	A	R	C	Z	T
S	D	O	T	R	D	E	T	N	E	L	A	T	H	Q	H	R	A	Q	E
V	W	X	O	E	W	Y	B	E	A	U	T	I	F	U	L	Y	O	B	D
K	A	F	S	D	E	R	O	V	A	F	G	K	D	R	U	Y	G	N	M

Word Bank

1. heir
2. special
3. royal
4. worthy
5. victorious
6. vessel
7. forgiven
8. chosen
9. adopted
10. precious
11. favored
12. smart
13. creation
14. crafted
15. gifted
16. blessed
17. treasured
18. loved
19. temple
20. beautiful
21. talented
22. complete
23. capable
24. intelligent
25. determined
26. honorable
27. wonderful

Crossword

Word Bank

Admire	Athlete	Defeat	Graceful
Afar	Beautiful	Degrade	Important
Alarm	Capable	Depict	Reflection
Amazing	Create	Divine	Shy
Assure	Declare	Embrace	Talented

Across

2. A mirrored image or shadow

5. To make certain

7. Someone who participates in sports

13. Something spectacular or larger than life

15. To look at someone with a special interest, a strong respect for someone

16. To win over something

19. Able to do or accomplish something

20. To make known

Down

1. Quite a distance

3. To have a special ability to do something well

4. To make something special and unique

6. Not bold or courageous

8. Forgiving and kind

9. Something quite extraordinary to behold, very pleasing to the eye

10. To make someone feel low or put down

11. To describe or paint a visible image

12. Something that is spiritual and sent by God

14. Very serious, comes with a sense of urgency

17. To hug or attach to someone

18. To frighten or make afraid

Coloring Page

Lesson 3 Activities

Cryptoquote Challenge

Fill in each blank with the corresponding letter that matches the number to reveal the hidden message.

$\underline{}\ \underline{}\quad \underline{}\ \underline{}\ \underline{}\ \underline{}\ \underline{}\ \underline{}\ ,\quad \underline{}\ \underline{}\ \underline{}\ \underline{}$

4   15   10   21   19   20   12   25 ,   12   15   22   5

13   5   18   3   25   1   14   4   8   21   13   2   12   25

23   1   12   11   23   9   20   8   7   15   4 .

KEY

A-1	F-6	K-11	P-16	U-21	Z-26
B-2	G-7	L-12	Q-17	V-22	
C-3	H-8	M-13	R-18	W-23	
D-4	I-9	N-14	S-19	X-24	
E-5	J-10	O-15	T-20	Y-25	

Word Search Challenge

Words can be found in any direction (including diagonals) and can overlap each other. Use the word bank below each challenge.

E	H	K	B	L	E	S	S	E	D	U	B	W	L	H	R	C	U	K	C
W	Z	W	O	U	K	W	R	O	Y	A	L	S	A	D	O	P	T	E	D
I	N	F	E	R	J	L	X	S	D	B	Q	H	M	V	Z	Z	N	C	E
T	N	R	L	I	C	I	T	E	L	A	I	C	E	P	S	X	O	R	T
G	R	T	C	E	R	B	D	Z	E	G	I	R	X	I	D	M	X	D	R
X	I	W	E	H	D	U	S	V	M	L	B	A	C	B	P	G	E	N	A
S	W	F	K	L	Z	Z	C	F	I	C	P	D	U	L	I	R	Z	C	M
X	I	S	T	Y	L	A	H	O	S	C	Y	M	E	O	U	Y	C	R	S
J	Q	P	R	E	C	I	O	U	S	T	T	T	E	S	T	M	A	E	Z
Q	L	Z	Y	B	D	O	G	W	R	U	E	O	A	T	I	R	N	A	D
T	O	C	M	C	X	C	C	E	L	C	O	E	R	Z	V	K	K	T	E
L	V	B	M	Z	H	X	A	U	N	Z	R	G	I	I	M	Y	X	I	N
L	E	S	S	E	V	O	F	P	N	T	I	O	H	R	O	P	O	O	I
L	D	Z	E	R	G	R	S	E	A	W	O	R	T	H	Y	U	W	N	M
O	A	P	Q	E	E	H	V	E	R	B	Q	E	H	J	N	D	S	A	R
I	K	Z	Z	D	N	I	O	I	N	E	L	B	A	R	O	N	O	H	E
Y	A	W	N	C	G	G	D	S	N	T	D	E	T	F	A	R	C	Z	T
S	D	O	T	R	D	E	T	N	E	L	A	T	H	Q	H	R	A	Q	E
V	W	X	O	E	W	Y	B	E	A	U	T	I	F	U	L	Y	O	B	D
K	A	F	S	D	E	R	O	V	A	F	G	K	D	R	U	Y	G	N	M

Word Bank

1. bondage	7. unequal	13. rules	19. justly
2. freedom	8. merciful	14. tragedy	20. commandment
3. police	9. fair	15. law	21. brutality
4. unkind	10. unfair	16. liberty	22. discrimination
5. prison	11. race	17. crime	
6. prayer	12. legal	18. matter	

Crossword

Word Bank

Ashamed   Elite   Injustice   Respect
Brutal   Exchange   Innocent   Roam
Cease   Fame   Involve   Sigh
Collaborate   Force   Realize   Trouble

Across

3. To wander or go a distance

5. To honor or treat with importance

9. To come together with ideas

10. Embarrassed, due to feelings of guilt

12. Join in with others, participate

14. To make something happen

15. Unfair actions or treatment

16. Pure, not guilty of wrongdoing

Down

1. Special group or high class, rich, wealthy

2. Mean, unkind

4. To stop or halt

6. To trade

7. To take special notice

8. To be viewed or seen as famous, stardom

11. To make or utter a sound

13. An unwanted circumstance that is hard to deal with

Coloring Page

Lesson 4 Activities

Hidden Images

Find the 20 hidden images in the coloring page below.

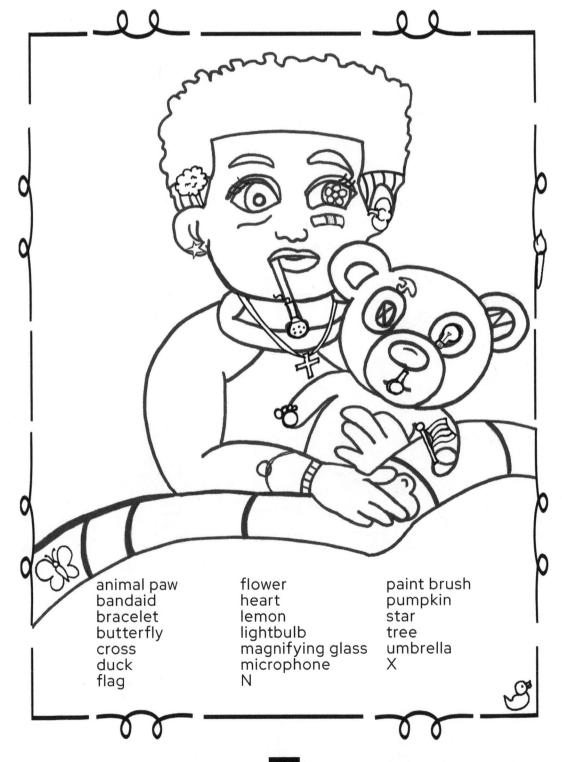

animal paw	flower	paint brush
bandaid	heart	pumpkin
bracelet	lemon	star
butterfly	lightbulb	tree
cross	magnifying glass	umbrella
duck	microphone	X
flag	N	

Word Search Challenge

Words can be found in any direction (including diagonals) and can overlap each other. Use the word bank below each challenge.

E	H	K	B	L	E	S	S	E	D	U	B	W	L	H	R	C	U	K	C
W	Z	W	O	U	K	W	R	O	Y	A	L	S	A	D	O	P	T	E	D
I	N	F	E	R	J	L	X	S	D	B	Q	H	M	V	Z	Z	N	C	E
T	N	R	L	I	C	I	T	E	L	A	I	C	E	P	S	X	O	R	T
G	R	T	C	E	R	B	D	Z	E	G	I	R	X	I	D	M	X	D	R
X	I	W	E	H	D	U	S	V	M	L	B	A	C	B	P	G	E	N	A
S	W	F	K	L	Z	Z	C	F	I	C	P	D	U	L	I	R	Z	C	M
X	I	S	T	Y	L	A	H	O	S	C	Y	M	E	O	U	Y	C	R	S
J	Q	P	R	E	C	I	O	U	S	T	T	T	E	S	T	M	A	E	Z
Q	L	Z	Y	B	D	O	G	W	R	U	E	O	A	T	I	R	N	A	D
T	O	C	M	C	X	C	C	E	L	C	O	E	R	Z	V	K	K	T	E
L	V	B	M	Z	H	X	A	U	N	Z	R	G	I	I	M	Y	X	I	N
L	E	S	S	E	V	O	F	P	N	T	I	O	H	R	O	P	O	O	I
L	D	Z	E	R	G	R	S	E	A	W	O	R	T	H	Y	U	W	N	M
O	A	P	Q	E	E	H	V	E	R	B	Q	E	H	J	N	D	S	A	R
I	K	Z	Z	D	N	I	O	I	N	E	L	B	A	R	O	N	O	H	E
Y	A	W	N	C	G	G	D	S	N	T	D	E	T	F	A	R	C	Z	T
S	D	O	T	R	D	E	T	N	E	L	A	T	H	Q	H	R	A	Q	E
V	W	X	O	E	W	Y	B	E	A	U	T	I	F	U	L	Y	O	B	D
K	A	F	S	D	E	R	O	V	A	F	G	K	D	R	U	Y	G	N	M

Word Bank

1. sick
2. pain
3. comforter
4. care
5. doctor
6. prayer
7. unsociable
8. alone
9. loved
10. nurse
11. patient
12. kind
13. deliverer
14. faith
15. medicine
16. isolated
17. hospital
18. fearful
19. joyful
20. confined
21. abandoned
22. healer

Crossword

Word Bank

Bartimaeus	Daughter	Lazarus	Peter
Blind	Deaf	Lepers	Pool
Blood	Epileptic	Mute	Unclean
Centurion	Lame	Paralytic	Widow

Across

2. State of the man's spirit in Mark 1:21

5. The brother of Mary and Martha (John 11:11)

9. Jairus's family member (Matthew 9:18)

10. Mother-in-law of which disciple? (Matthew 8:14)

13. Place where the man was healed in Bethesda (John 5:2)

14. People who could not walk

15. Title of the soldier healed in Matthew 8:5

16. Person whose son was healed in Luke 7:11

Down

1. Malady of the ten men healed at the same time (Luke 17:11)

3. Blind man in Matthew 20:29

4. People who could not hear

6. People who could not talk (Matthew 9:32)

7. The man who couldn't walk (Matthew 9:1)

8. Illness of the boy mentioned in Matthew 17:14

11. People who could not see (Matthew 9:27)

12. What the woman in Matthew 9:20 suffered from, the issue of ...

Crossword

Word Bank

Alone	Compassion	Display	Sick
Approach	Consistently	Gratitude	Strategic
Assignment	Creature	Organize	Uplift
Commitment	Defeated	Reliable	Virtual

Across

3. To come near

5. Physically ill, not in good health

7. An animated character

9. Not in person

12. To put on showcase

13. To be present or there when in need

14. Orderly, to put in place

15. To show up and be available, dedicated

16. To show sympathy or concern

Down

1. To act with a clear plan

2. Always, frequently or regularly occurring

4. To take a loss, fail at winning

6. To feel thankful

8. By one's self, lonely

10. Work or duty

11. To make or lift one's spirits

Jesus[1] and Me Poster

Draw yourself in the box.

For God so loved _____ that He gave His Son, Jesus,
to die for me.   (insert your name)

(John 3:16)

——————

1   Jesus image source: http://cliparts.co/cliparts/6Tr/8y9/6Tr8y98TK.jpg

Coloring Page

Lesson 5 Activities

Cryptoquote Challenge

Fill in each blank with the corresponding letter that matches the number to reveal the hidden message.

1. Moses and his family were born in ___ ___ ___ ___ ___ .
                                                5   7   25 16 20

2. He was an ___ ___ ___ ___ ___ ___ ___ ___ ___ who had been adopted
                    9 19 18 1 5 **12** **9** **20** **5**

   by Pharoah's ___ ___ ___ ___ ___ ___ ___ ___ .
                           4   1 21 7 8 20 5 18

3. His adoptive mother's name was ___ ___ ___ ___ ___ ___ .
                                   2 9 20 9 1 **5**

4. She found baby Moses in the ___ ___ ___ ___ River.
                         14 9 12 5

5. Moses was later led by God to set his ___ ___ ___ ___ ___ ___ **free.**
                          16 5 15 16 12 **5**

___ ___ ___ ___ ___ ___ ___ ___ ___ ___ ___ ___ ___ ___ .
22 5 14 7 5 14 3 5   9 19   13 9 14 4

___ ___ ___ ___ ___ ___ ___ ___ ___ ___ ___ .
19 1 25 19   20 8 5   **12** 15 18 4

KEY

A-1	F-6	K-11	P-16	U-21	Z-26
B-2	G-7	L-12	Q-17	V-22	
C-3	H-8	M-13	R-18	W-23	
D-4	I-9	N-14	S-19	X-24	
E-5	J-10	O-15	T-20	Y-25	

Word Search Challenge

Words can be found in any direction (including diagonals) and can overlap each other. Use the word bank below each challenge.

M	Q	S	U	L	Z	K	X	O	R	I	X	Q	N	E	S	O	H	C	F
Q	D	D	L	Z	P	L	A	I	C	E	P	S	C	G	S	E	S	O	M
D	K	Q	E	P	U	R	P	O	S	E	N	C	H	L	R	C	K	R	L
Q	E	A	S	J	I	R	Y	Q	R	R	U	I	O	L	M	J	N	T	
X	H	N	M	V	A	W	D	L	P	Q	B	M	L	V	Z	N	G	H	Z
O	D	C	O	P	X	L	I	I	S	Z	X	B	D	E	O	Z	T	B	Z
Q	E	B	Y	I	N	C	P	M	K	W	K	R	O	D	X	P	I	X	D
N	T	N	K	W	T	S	S	A	X	P	Z	E	F	B	B	K	N	I	N
P	N	V	D	V	J	I	D	F	S	T	W	H	G	V	R	B	V	J	D
U	I	I	W	Y	U	I	S	B	G	U	L	T	O	O	O	I	Z	A	O
I	O	N	L	Z	H	A	P	O	D	U	B	A	D	R	N	F	J	K	H
V	P	L	N	K	T	T	F	T	P	L	H	F	N	E	B	C	J	D	O
F	P	C	H	I	L	D	R	E	N	V	S	B	Y	F	S	R	E	D	G
I	A	L	B	A	U	I	A	O	X	R	I	B	T	S	P	O	K	V	B
W	E	M	D	I	M	K	O	X	W	R	J	L	V	X	P	L	T	N	L
B	M	O	T	H	E	R	I	Z	T	Y	B	T	P	O	D	A	N	A	Y
L	B	P	N	S	J	R	B	H	M	C	E	T	I	N	U	N	Q	H	W
S	C	R	I	G	I	M	Y	Z	W	B	E	L	O	N	G	U	V	P	L
W	Q	W	A	N	T	E	D	D	P	U	K	I	V	G	Q	J	D	R	T
J	M	D	E	S	T	I	N	E	D	I	A	F	N	H	Z	V	C	O	X

Word Bank

1. loved
2. birth
3. special
4. born
5. worthy
6. placed
7. adopt
8. orphan
9. mother
10. child of God
11. purpose
12. unite
13. children
14. Moses
15. divine
16. positioned
17. destined
18. appointed
19. belong
20. father
21. family
22. chosen
23. wanted

Crossword

Word Bank

Abuse   Currently   Observe   Tease
Appear   Desperate   Patient   Unease
Assure   Fright   Polite
Brilliant   Legitimate   Routine
Challenge   Neglect   Succeed

Across

4. Uncomfortable or restless

5. To be calm while waiting

6. Regularly, daily habits or schedule

8. A test or something difficult to handle

13. To watch or take notice

14. To win and accomplish in the game of life

15. To make fun of or pick on

17. In real need, a sense of urgency

Down

1. To be kind or courteous

2. To make certain

3. To be scared, afraid or spooked

7. To fail to take care of another's needs

9. Smart, capable, outstanding

10. Bad or hurtful treatment

11. Real, necessary, something of importance

12. Happening now

16. To show up

Coloring Page

Lesson 6 Activities

Words can be found in any direction (including diagonals) and can overlap each other. Use the word bank below each challenge.

Word Search Challenge

M	Q	S	U	L	Z	K	X	O	R	I	X	Q	N	E	S	O	H	C	F
Q	D	D	L	Z	P	L	A	I	C	E	P	S	C	G	S	E	S	O	M
D	K	Q	E	P	U	R	P	O	S	E	N	C	H	L	R	C	K	R	L
Q	E	A	S	C	J	I	R	Y	Q	R	R	U	I	O	L	M	J	N	T
X	H	N	M	V	A	W	D	L	P	Q	B	M	L	V	Z	N	G	H	Z
O	D	C	O	P	X	L	I	I	S	Z	X	B	D	E	O	Z	T	B	Z
Q	E	B	Y	I	N	C	P	M	K	W	K	R	O	D	X	P	I	X	D
N	T	N	K	W	T	S	S	A	X	P	Z	E	F	B	B	K	N	I	N
P	N	V	D	V	J	I	D	F	S	T	W	H	G	V	R	B	V	J	D
U	I	I	W	Y	U	I	S	B	G	U	L	T	O	O	O	I	Z	A	O
I	O	N	L	Z	H	A	P	O	D	U	B	A	D	R	N	F	J	K	H
V	P	L	N	K	T	T	F	T	P	L	H	F	N	E	B	C	J	D	O
F	P	C	H	I	L	D	R	E	N	V	S	B	Y	F	S	R	E	D	G
I	A	L	B	A	U	I	A	O	X	R	I	B	T	S	P	O	K	V	B
W	E	M	D	I	M	K	O	X	W	R	J	L	V	X	P	L	T	N	L
B	M	O	T	H	E	R	I	Z	T	Y	B	T	P	O	D	A	N	A	Y
L	B	P	N	S	J	R	B	H	M	C	E	T	I	N	U	N	Q	H	W
S	C	R	I	G	I	M	Y	Z	W	B	E	L	O	N	G	U	V	P	L
W	Q	W	A	N	T	E	D	D	P	U	K	I	V	G	Q	J	D	R	T
J	M	D	E	S	T	I	N	E	D	I	A	F	N	H	Z	V	C	O	X

Word Bank

1. troubled
2. training
3. cruelty
4. exasperate
5. mean
6. neglect
7. restore
8. prevention
9. control
10. precious
11. discipline
12. loved
13. mistreated
14. unkind
15. anger
16. separated
17. self-control
18. chaos
19. painful
20. abuse
21. frightened
22. abandoned

Crossword

Word Bank

Adore | Eventually | Ordeal | Threaten
Bail | Fearful | Protect | Violence
Boisterous | Heal | Recover | Witnessed
Comfort | Material | Strife
Demonstrate | Mend | Suffer

Across

4. To complete in a matter of time

6. To show or illustrate

8. To make payment to get out of jail

12. To repair or get better

13. Acts that leads to aggression or verbal and physical outbursts

14. Very loud, alarming, noisy

16. To keep safe

17. Very frightened, or afraid

Down

1. To care deeply or admire

2. To make well again

3. Items needed to complete a task

5. To be made to feel unsafe

7. A big matter to attend to or deal with

9. To experience lots of pain

10. To make someone feel better, easy

11. To see and observe something taking place

15. To get better, bounce back

Coloring Page

Lesson 7 Activities

Word Search Challenge

Words can be found in any direction (including diagonals) and can overlap each other. Use the word bank below each challenge.

M	Q	S	U	L	Z	K	X	O	R	I	X	Q	N	E	S	O	H	C	F
Q	D	D	L	Z	P	L	A	I	C	E	P	S	C	G	S	E	S	O	M
D	K	Q	E	P	U	R	P	O	S	E	N	C	H	L	R	C	K	R	L
Q	E	A	S	C	J	I	R	Y	Q	R	R	U	I	O	L	M	J	N	T
X	H	N	M	V	A	W	D	L	P	Q	B	M	L	V	Z	N	G	H	Z
O	D	C	O	P	X	L	I	I	S	Z	X	B	D	E	O	Z	T	B	Z
Q	E	B	Y	I	N	C	P	M	K	W	K	R	O	D	X	P	I	X	D
N	T	N	K	W	T	S	S	A	X	P	Z	E	F	B	B	K	N	I	N
P	N	V	D	V	J	I	D	F	S	T	W	H	G	V	R	B	V	J	D
U	I	I	W	Y	U	I	S	B	G	U	L	T	O	O	O	I	Z	A	O
I	O	N	L	Z	H	A	P	O	D	U	B	A	D	R	N	F	J	K	H
V	P	L	N	K	T	T	F	T	P	L	H	F	N	E	B	C	J	D	O
F	P	C	H	I	L	D	R	E	N	V	S	B	Y	F	S	R	E	D	G
I	A	L	B	A	U	I	A	O	X	R	I	B	T	S	P	O	K	V	B
W	E	M	D	I	M	K	O	X	W	R	J	L	V	X	P	L	T	N	L
B	M	O	T	H	E	R	I	Z	T	Y	B	T	P	O	D	A	N	A	Y
L	B	P	N	S	J	R	B	H	M	C	E	T	I	N	U	N	Q	H	W
S	C	R	I	G	I	M	Y	Z	W	B	E	L	O	N	G	U	V	P	L
W	Q	W	A	N	T	E	D	D	P	U	K	I	V	G	Q	J	D	R	T
J	M	D	E	S	T	I	N	E	D	I	A	F	N	H	Z	V	C	O	X

Word Bank

1. stop
2. Esther
3. dysfunctional
4. harm
5. mental
6. verbal
7. help
8. bully
9. assist
10. unkind
11. hit
12. attack
13. mean
14. Daniel
15. internal
16. intentional
17. rude
18. physical
19. words
20. brutal
21. repetition
22. hurtful
23. report

Crossword

Word Bank

Absent
Boldness
Bully
Deal

Defeat
Emotions
Encourage
Ferocious

Miserable
Problem
Punish
Regardless

Reveal
Wreck

Across

3. To make one happy or feel better

4. To experience painful consequences based on bad actions

7. To act with courage

9. To trade or swap with someone else

13. To make one unhappy or uncomfortable

14. To be mean and forceful

Down

1. A collection of feelings

2. Careless, to act without thinking

5. Mean and rude

6. To make known

8. To lose or fail to win

10. To make a ruin or mess of

11. Not present

12. To be unruly or uncooperative

Coloring Page

Lesson 8 Activities

Word Search Challenge

Words can be found in any direction (including diagonals) and can overlap each other. Use the word bank below each challenge.

M	Q	S	U	L	Z	K	X	O	R	I	X	Q	N	E	S	O	H	C	F
Q	D	D	L	Z	P	L	A	I	C	E	P	S	C	G	S	E	S	O	M
D	K	Q	E	P	U	R	P	O	S	E	N	C	H	L	R	C	K	R	L
Q	E	A	S	C	J	I	R	Y	Q	R	R	U	I	O	L	M	J	N	T
X	H	N	M	V	A	W	D	L	P	Q	B	M	L	V	Z	N	G	H	Z
O	D	C	O	P	X	L	I	I	S	Z	X	B	D	E	O	Z	T	B	Z
Q	E	B	Y	I	N	C	P	M	K	W	K	R	O	D	X	P	I	X	D
N	T	N	K	W	T	S	S	A	X	P	Z	E	F	B	B	K	N	I	N
P	N	V	D	V	J	I	D	F	S	T	W	H	G	V	R	B	V	J	D
U	I	I	W	Y	U	I	S	B	G	U	L	T	O	O	O	I	Z	A	O
I	O	N	L	Z	H	A	P	O	D	U	B	A	D	R	N	F	J	K	H
V	P	L	N	K	T	T	F	T	P	L	H	F	N	E	B	C	J	D	O
F	P	C	H	I	L	D	R	E	N	V	S	B	Y	F	S	R	E	D	G
I	A	L	B	A	U	I	A	O	X	R	I	B	T	S	P	O	K	V	B
W	E	M	D	I	M	K	O	X	W	R	J	L	V	X	P	L	T	N	L
B	M	O	T	H	E	R	I	Z	T	Y	B	T	P	O	D	A	N	A	Y
L	B	P	N	S	J	R	B	H	M	C	E	T	I	N	U	N	Q	H	W
S	C	R	I	G	I	M	Y	Z	W	B	E	L	O	N	G	U	V	P	L
W	Q	W	A	N	T	E	D	D	P	U	K	I	V	G	Q	J	D	R	T
J	M	D	E	S	T	I	N	E	D	I	A	F	N	H	Z	V	C	O	X

Word Bank

1. cross
2. grace
3. victorious
4. grave
5. crucifixion
6. lamb
7. eternal
8. celebration
9. confess
10. blood
11. penalty
12. gift
13. Jesus
14. gap
15. resurrection
16. sin
17. die
18. love
19. forgiven
20. separated
21. provision
22. Easter
23. sacrifice
24. reunited
25. eternal life

Crossword

Word Bank

Debt	Extraordinary	Redeem	Transform
Decision	Forewarn	Restore	Victory
Deliver	Miraculous	Sacrifice	
Embrace	Prophet	Signify	
Eternally	Receive	Sin	

Across

4. To accept payment for something owed

6. To make known by using signs

10. To hug or eagerly accept

11. To decide, act or make up one's mind

12. To bring back to the original state

13. Someone who tells the truth

14. To change

16. Something out of the normal

17. To drop or save from danger or harm

Down

1. Something being offered for someone else

2. A bill or payment owed

3. To make known before time or in advance

5. Something out of the ordinary

7. To win or experience gain

8. To do wrong or break the law

9. Everlasting, never ending

15. To buy back or make payment

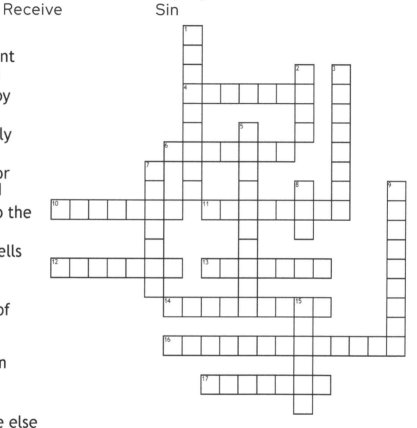

Coloring Page 1

Coloring Page 2

Lesson 9 Activities

Word Search Challenge

Words can be found in any direction (including diagonals) and can overlap each other. Use the word bank below each challenge.

M	Q	S	U	L	Z	K	X	O	R	I	X	Q	N	E	S	O	H	C	F
Q	D	D	L	Z	P	L	A	I	C	E	P	S	C	G	S	E	S	O	M
D	K	Q	E	P	U	R	P	O	S	E	N	C	H	L	R	C	K	R	L
Q	E	A	S	C	J	I	R	Y	Q	R	R	U	I	O	L	M	J	N	T
X	H	N	M	V	A	W	D	L	P	Q	B	M	L	V	Z	N	G	H	Z
O	D	C	O	P	X	L	I	I	S	Z	X	B	D	E	O	Z	T	B	Z
Q	E	B	Y	I	N	C	P	M	K	W	K	R	O	D	X	P	I	X	D
N	T	N	K	W	T	S	S	A	X	P	Z	E	F	B	B	K	N	I	N
P	N	V	D	V	J	I	D	F	S	T	W	H	G	V	R	B	V	J	D
U	I	I	W	Y	U	I	S	B	G	U	L	T	O	O	O	I	Z	A	O
I	O	N	L	Z	H	A	P	O	D	U	B	A	D	R	N	F	J	K	H
V	P	L	N	K	T	T	F	T	P	L	H	F	N	E	B	C	J	D	O
F	P	C	H	I	L	D	R	E	N	V	S	B	Y	F	S	R	E	D	G
I	A	L	B	A	U	I	A	O	X	R	I	B	T	S	P	O	K	V	B
W	E	M	D	I	M	K	O	X	W	R	J	L	V	X	P	L	T	N	L
B	M	O	T	H	E	R	I	Z	T	Y	B	T	P	O	D	A	N	A	Y
L	B	P	N	S	J	R	B	H	M	C	E	T	I	N	U	N	Q	H	W
S	C	R	I	G	I	M	Y	Z	W	B	E	L	O	N	G	U	V	P	L
W	Q	W	A	N	T	E	D	D	P	U	K	I	V	G	Q	J	D	R	T
J	M	D	E	S	T	I	N	E	D	I	A	F	N	H	Z	V	C	O	X

Word Bank

1. storyteller
2. family
3. nurturer
4. responsible
5. mom
6. chauffeur
7. Proverbs
8. hard
9. nurse
10. Shero
11. mother
12. God's vessel
13. wife
14. kind
15. cook
16. loving
17. worker
18. caregiver
19. teacher
20. counselor
21. priorities

Crossword

Word Bank

Assure	Failure	Provide	Struggle
Cheap	Finances	Rejoice	Tease
Depend	Frequent	Rely	Tirelessly
Dread	Income	Source	
Evicted	Mercy	Stable	

Across

2. To not accomplish a goal, dream or desire

4. Happen often

5. Forced to move

9. Something you can depend on

10. Not expensive

11. Depend on

13. Someone you can count on

16. One's money or income

17. Stay in place without movement or change

18. Try hard

Down

1. Work hard without rest

3. Give to a person in need

6. Extended kindness

7. Make fun of

8. Not look forward to

12. Celebrate a victory

14. Money, salary earned for a job performed

15. Encourage or make one believe

Coloring Page

Lesson 10 Activities

Word Search Challenge

Words can be found in any direction (including diagonals) and can overlap each other. Use the word bank below each challenge.

M	Q	S	U	L	Z	K	X	O	R	I	X	Q	N	E	S	O	H	C	F
Q	D	D	L	Z	P	L	A	I	C	E	P	S	C	G	S	E	S	O	M
D	K	Q	E	P	U	R	P	O	S	E	N	C	H	L	R	C	K	R	L
Q	E	A	S	C	J	I	R	Y	Q	R	R	U	I	O	L	M	J	N	T
X	H	N	M	V	A	W	D	L	P	Q	B	M	L	V	Z	N	G	H	Z
O	D	C	O	P	X	L	I	I	S	Z	X	B	D	E	O	Z	T	B	Z
Q	E	B	Y	I	N	C	P	M	K	W	K	R	O	D	X	P	I	X	D
N	T	N	K	W	T	S	S	A	X	P	Z	E	F	B	B	K	N	I	N
P	N	V	D	V	J	I	D	F	S	T	W	H	G	V	R	B	V	J	D
U	I	I	W	Y	U	I	S	B	G	U	L	T	O	O	O	I	Z	A	O
I	O	N	L	Z	H	A	P	O	D	U	B	A	D	R	N	F	J	K	H
V	P	L	N	K	T	T	F	T	P	L	H	F	N	E	B	C	J	D	O
F	P	C	H	I	L	D	R	E	N	V	S	B	Y	F	S	R	E	D	G
I	A	L	B	A	U	I	A	O	X	R	I	B	T	S	P	O	K	V	B
W	E	M	D	I	M	K	O	X	W	R	J	L	V	X	P	L	T	N	L
B	M	O	T	H	E	R	I	Z	T	Y	B	T	P	O	D	A	N	A	Y
L	B	P	N	S	J	R	B	H	M	C	E	T	I	N	U	N	Q	H	W
S	C	R	I	G	I	M	Y	Z	W	B	E	L	O	N	G	U	V	P	L
W	Q	W	A	N	T	E	D	D	P	U	K	I	V	G	Q	J	D	R	T
J	M	D	E	S	T	I	N	E	D	I	A	F	N	H	Z	V	C	O	X

Word Bank

1. resourceful
2. disciplinarian
3. friend
4. father
5. kind
6. away
7. loyal
8. absent
9. Abba
10. shepherd
11. dependable
12. loving
13. good
14. God
15. provider
16. security
17. omnipresent
18. disconnected
19. protector
20. trustworthy

Crossword

Word Bank

Abandonment	Depart	Peers	Usher
Adhere	Drastically	Reject	Void
Affection	Frequent	Struggle	Warning
Cherish	Intelligent	Support	
Consult	Mend	Tirelessly	

Across

4. To leave or depart, failing to return

6. To bring in or lead to

7. To hold dear or treat very special

10. To show or express love and care

13. To give or provide help or assistance

16. Work or labor until one becomes exhausted

17. To turn away from, or fail to accept

18. Very smart

Down

1. To make better, heal, recover

2. To stick with or follow

3. Sudden change

5. To leave or exit

8. To battle with effort, something hard or challenging

9. Talk with or make something known

11. Empty

12. To treat with caution or make aware

14. Someone you share something in common (age, status, or ability)

15. To do often or a lot

Coloring Page

Lesson 11 Activities

Word Search Challenge

Words can be found in any direction (including diagonals) and can overlap each other. Use the word bank below each challenge.

M	Q	S	U	L	Z	K	X	O	R	I	X	Q	N	E	S	O	H	C	F
Q	D	D	L	Z	P	L	A	I	C	E	P	S	C	G	S	E	S	O	M
D	K	Q	E	P	U	R	P	O	S	E	N	C	H	L	R	C	K	R	L
Q	E	A	S	C	J	I	R	Y	Q	R	R	U	I	O	L	M	J	N	T
X	H	N	M	V	A	W	D	L	P	Q	B	M	L	V	Z	N	G	H	Z
O	D	C	O	P	X	L	I	I	S	Z	X	B	D	E	O	Z	T	B	Z
Q	E	B	Y	I	N	C	P	M	K	W	K	R	O	D	X	P	I	X	D
N	T	N	K	W	T	S	S	A	X	P	Z	E	F	B	B	K	N	I	N
P	N	V	D	V	J	I	D	F	S	T	W	H	G	V	R	B	V	J	D
U	I	I	W	Y	U	I	S	B	G	U	L	T	O	O	O	I	Z	A	O
I	O	N	L	Z	H	A	P	O	D	U	B	A	D	R	N	F	J	K	H
V	P	L	N	K	T	T	F	T	P	L	H	F	N	E	B	C	J	D	O
F	P	C	H	I	L	D	R	E	N	V	S	B	Y	F	S	R	E	D	G
I	A	L	B	A	U	I	A	O	X	R	I	B	T	S	P	O	K	V	B
W	E	M	D	I	M	K	O	X	W	R	J	L	V	X	P	L	T	N	L
B	M	O	T	H	E	R	I	Z	T	Y	B	T	P	O	D	A	N	A	Y
L	B	P	N	S	J	R	B	H	M	C	E	T	I	N	U	N	Q	H	W
S	C	R	I	G	I	M	Y	Z	W	B	E	L	O	N	G	U	V	P	L
W	Q	W	A	N	T	E	D	D	P	U	K	I	V	G	Q	J	D	R	T
J	M	D	E	S	T	I	N	E	D	I	A	F	N	H	Z	V	C	O	X

Word Bank

1. tearless	8. mansion	15. united	22. magnificent
2. pleasant	9. calm	16. oneness	23. pearly gates
3. painless	10. unimaginable	17. serene	24. second coming
4. throne	11. heaven	18. beautiful	25. peaceful
5. golden	12. joyful	19. marvelous	26. palatial
6. completion	13. healed	20. glorious	27. presence
7. Jesus	14. eternal	21. enjoyable	of God

Crossword

Across

2. The reason we exist for accomplishing something great

3. Unable to part or be away from one another

6. Watch or take notice

8. The place where we will see God

10. Strong desire to do something

11. Full of joy

14. Strong affection

16. Recommend as important

17. Tell or show

18. Very serious

Down

1. Medicine or procedure needed for a cure

4. Show off to others

5. Deep hurt and longing

7. Lasting mark

9. Emptiness or deep hole

12. Not wanted

13. Lift one's spirit and make feel better

15. Hug or show affection

Coloring Page

Charity's Leader Resources.

Lesson 1

FLOWER PETAL TEMPLATE

On each petal write out a character trait that makes you a good friend. (ex. Kind, caring, honest, etc.) Write your name in the circle in the middle. They can also use this to fill in the petals of their flowers.

Lesson 2

Leaders: After lesson 2, give each child a copy and have them place in their bibles or on their wall as a reminder of who they are.

Lesson 2 cont.

GOD'S MIRROR

Write in the mirror what God says about you.

Lesson 4

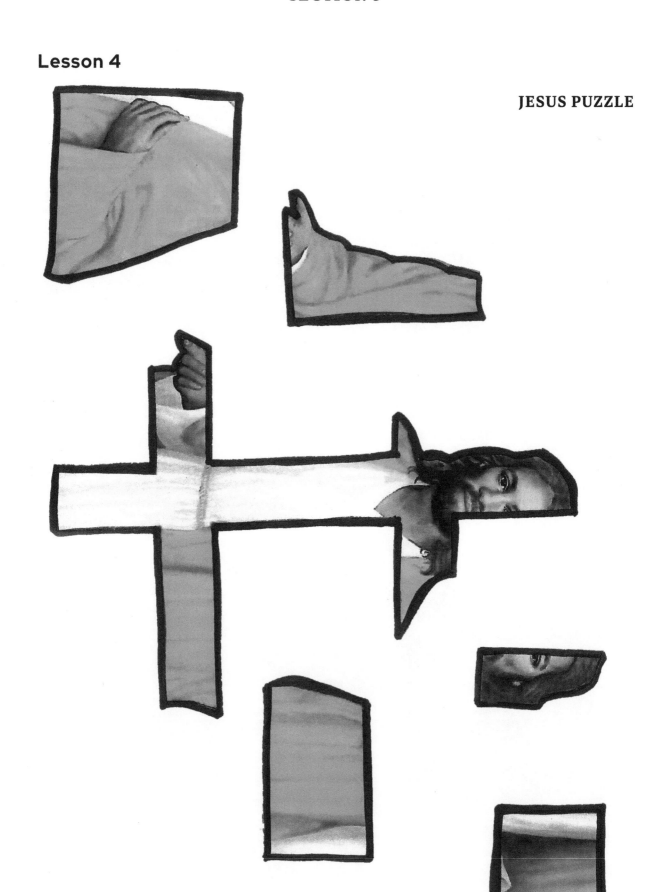

Jesus Puzzle

ANSWER KEY

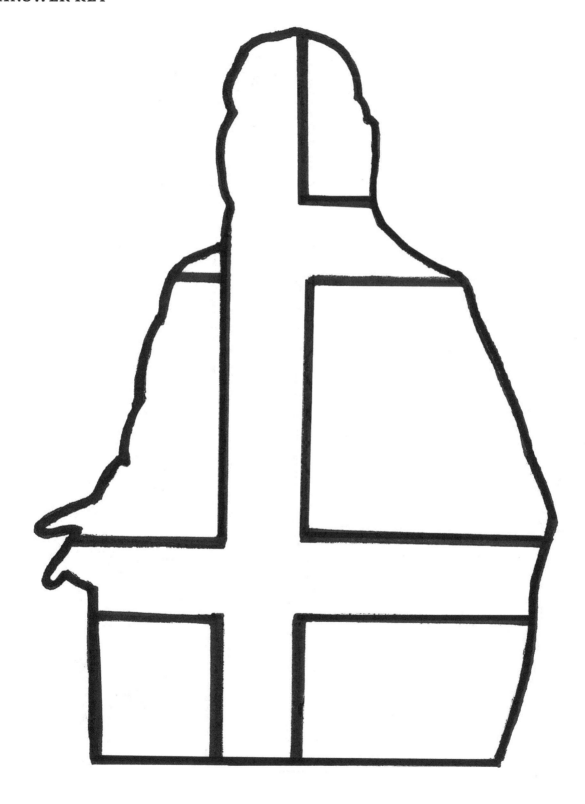

Lesson 6

EMOTIONAL WHEEL

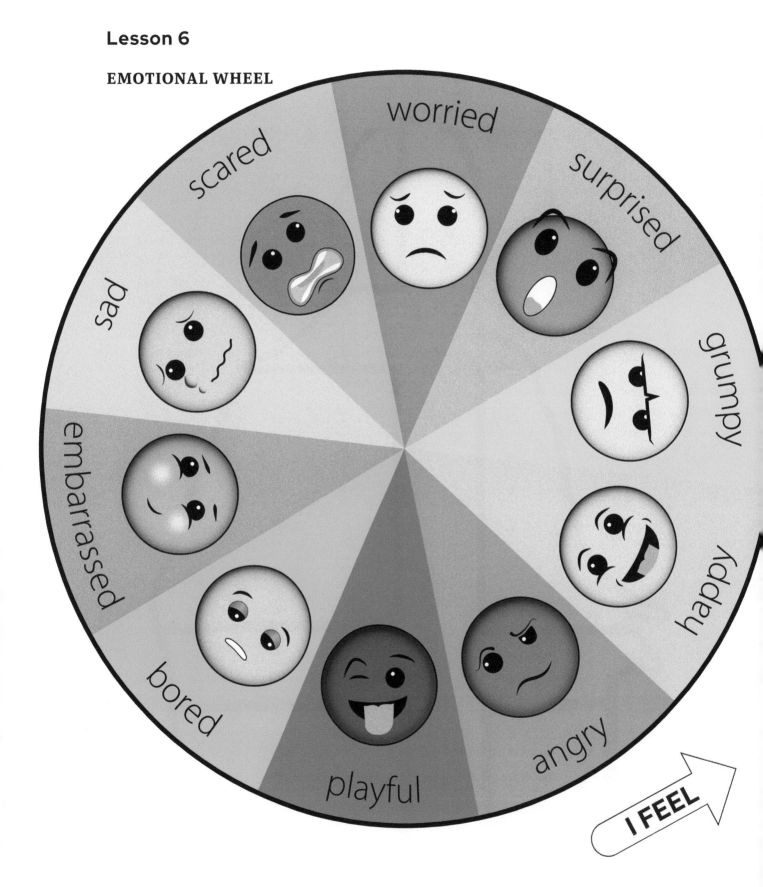

Lesson 7

PROBLEM SOLVING WHEEL

PATH TO SAFETY

STAY CALM

STAND PROUD

SAY STOP IT!

MOVE AWAY

GO TELL

CHARACTERS

SECTION 3

PATH TO SAFETY ACTIVITY BOARD

Ask students to position each character according to the described scenario.

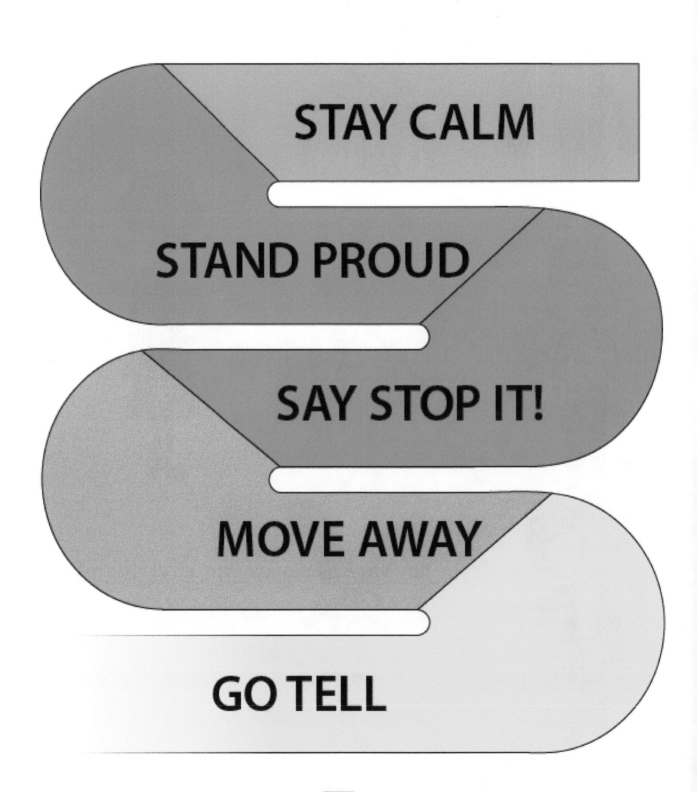

Have children place the characters in their choice of positions.

Teasing

- Everyone is having fun
- No one is getting hurt physically or mentally
- Everyone is participating equally to the disagreement

Conflict

- No one is having fun
- There is a possible solution
- Equal balance of power

Mean Moment

- Someone is being hurt on purpose either physically or mentally
- Reaction to a strong feeling or emotion
- An isolated event (doesn't happen regularly)

Bullying

- Someone is being mean on purpose
- Repetitive (happens regularly)
- Imbalance of power

Print the poster for display or sharing

Teasing

- Everyone is having fun
- No one is getting hurt physically or mentally
- Everyone is partici-pating equally to the disagreement

Conflict

- No one is having fun
- There is a possible solution
- Equal balance of power

Mean Moment

- Someone is being hurt on purpose either physically or mentally
- Reaction to a strong feeling or emotion
- An isolated event (doesn't happen regularly)

Bullying

- Someone is being mean on purpose
- Repetitive (happens regularly)
- Imbalance of power

Lesson 10

PRAYER CUBE TEMPLATE

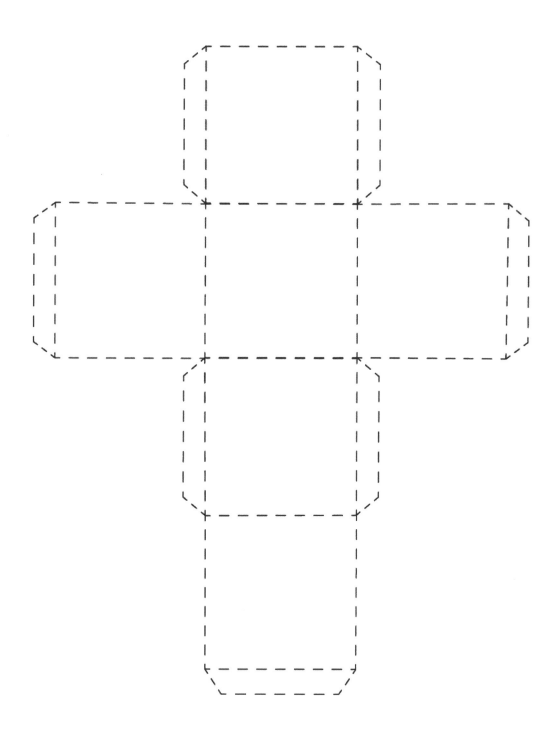

Lesson 11

BRIDGING THE GAP POSTER

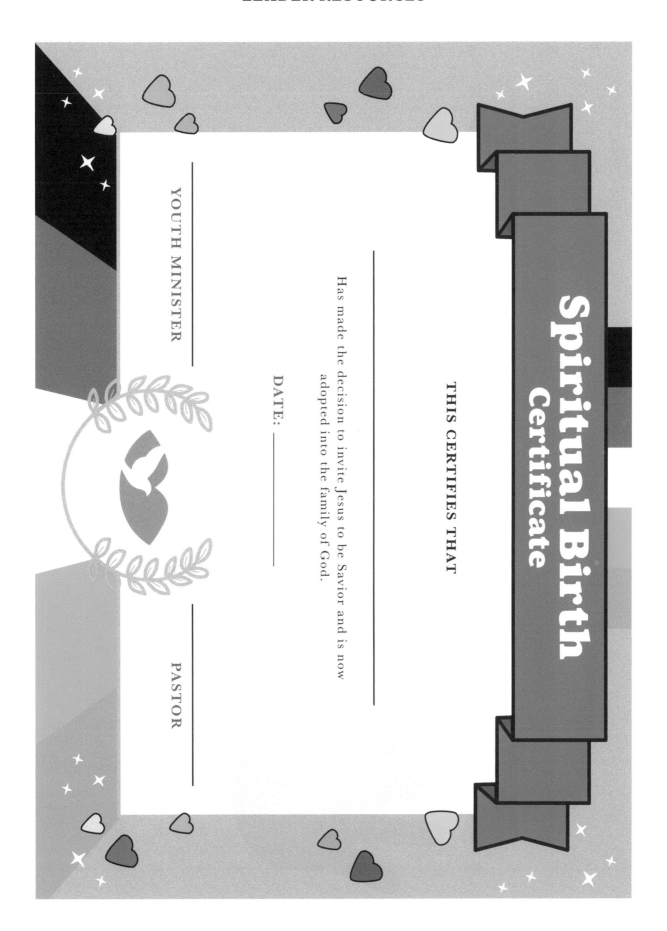

Spiritual Birth
Certificate

THIS CERTIFIES THAT

_____

Has made the decision to invite Jesus to be Savior and is now adopted into the family of God.

DATE: _____

YOUTH MINISTER _____

PASTOR _____

9 781950 075874